THE TASTE OF
FRANCE

GALLERY BOOKS
An Imprint of W. H. Smith Publishers Inc.
112 Madison Avenue
New York City 10016

Compiled by Frédéric Lebain and Jean-Paul Paireault
Photographed by Jean-Paul Paireault
Designed by Philip Clucas
Adapted and Translated by Lynn Jennings-Collombet

Acknowledgements

The publishers would like to thank the following for their
valuable assistance and cooperation in the production of
this book:

Madame Bayle, at Mas Le Plan in Lourmarin, for facilities for
location photography.
The shopkeepers of Lourmarin and Pertuis for their special
efforts to obtain and provide a variety of fresh and attractive
fish, meats and general provisions.
Morcrette, and Villeroy and Boch for the loan of glassware
and plates.
Cine Photo Provence, in Aix-en-Provence for film processing.
Kettie Artigaud for her help with general styling and
furnishing.
Kathleen Jennings for her patience and help throughout the
adaptation and translation of this book.
Monsieur Remande, director of l'Ecole Supérieure de
Cuisine in Paris.
Chef Xavier Vallero and Chef Eric Trochon for permission
to use a selection of their recipes.
Also to Monsieur and Madame Lebain, Monsieur David and
Madame Marie-Solange Bezaunt, Madame Chardot, and
Monsieur Bernard Bouton of Sougé.

CLB 2194
This edition first published in the United States in 1989 by Gallery Books,
an imprint of W.H. Smith Publishers, Inc.,
112 Madison Avenue, New York 10016
© 1989 Colour Library Books Ltd., Godalming, Surrey, England
Typesetting by Words and Spaces, Rowlands Castle, Hants, England
Color separations by Hong Kong Graphic Arts Ltd., Hong Kong
All rights reserved
ISBN 0 8317 53564 3

Gallery Books are available for bulk purchase for sales promotions and
premium use. For details write or telephone the Manager of Special
Sales, W.H. Smith Publishers, Inc.,
112 Madison Avenue, New York, New York 10016. (212) 532-6600

· THE TASTE OF ·
FRANCE

Frederic Lebain · Jean-Paul Paireault

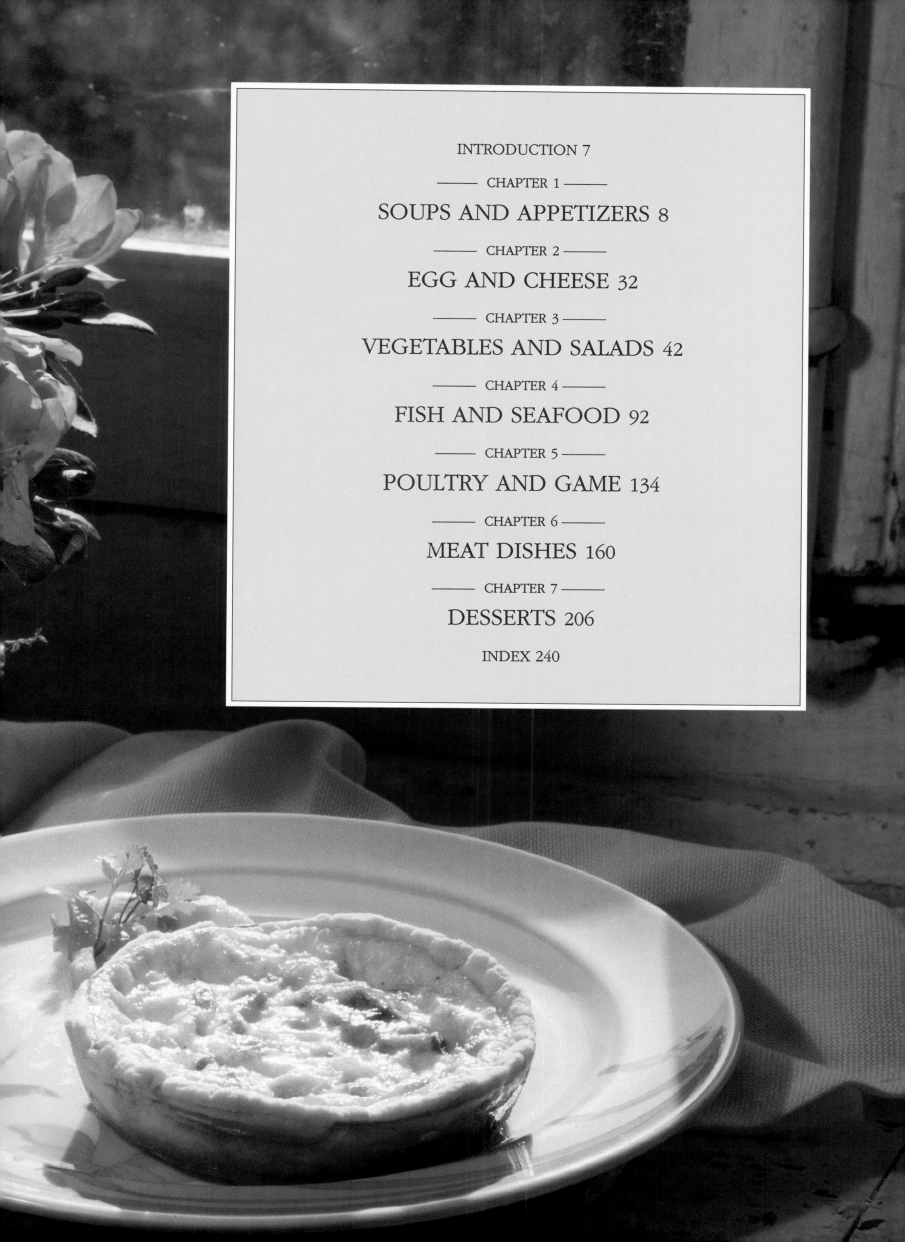

Introduction

The words "food" and "France" are almost synonymous. In no other country in the world does cooking have such a mystique as it does in France. Cooking is an art here, and not only in the *haute cuisine* restaurants of Paris. In fact, good food is such a part of ordinary, everyday life that the most famous and best-loved dishes are those that come from humble origins. For example, think of country pâtés, redolent of herbs, garlic and brandy; rich stews; hearty soups, and desserts made with pears, cherries or strawberries – the produce of local orchards and gardens.

Even though France has been reorganized into *départements*, the old provincial names – Normandy, Brittany, Champagne, the Loire, Ile-de-France, Alsace Lorraine, Burgundy, Bordeaux, Franche-Comté, Languedoc, Roussillon and Provence – still have special meaning where French cooking is concerned.

From Normandy, on the north coast, comes the richest milk, cream and butter. The province grows no wine, but its orchards produce cider apples from which Calvados, a fiery brandy, is made. Cider is a favorite drink, too, and dishes that combine it with apples and cream often bear the name "Normande."

Brittany's lambs graze on salt marshes, which gives their meat a distinctive flavor and forms the basis for a famous dish of roast or braised lamb with haricot beans. The region's best-known contribution, however, has to be crêpes. These thin pancakes are served with a variety of fillings, from cheese and ham to mixtures of local seafood.

The Champagne region has made a memorable gastronomic contribution – the world's most celebrated sparkling wine. The province is also known for its rich dishes with a Flemish influence and for a delicious savory version of choux pastry called a *gougère*.

A lovely, fragrant wine comes from the Alsace region which, with its neighbor Lorraine, shares a fondness for hearty food that is very German in character. Foie gras and the rich pâté made from it are also produced here, and to drink there are varieties of eau de vie – kirsch, mirabelle and framboise, made from cherries, plums and raspberries, respectively.

The Loire flows through the heart of France. Walled kitchen gardens grow vegetables and herbs almost all the year round, while the vineyards produce delicate wines that complement the food of the region perfectly. The famous sauce, beurre blanc, a liaison of white wine, shallots and butter, originated here long before the *nouvelle cuisine* movement made it popular.

Ile-de-France, with Paris at its center, is where *haute cuisine* was born. Because fine restaurants are what everyone thinks of first when visiting this region, its other assets are sometimes taken for granted. In the countryside surrounding Paris, hunting game is still very popular, and cooking it is an art. Mushrooms, both wild and cultivated, grow abundantly here, as do strawberries, while the rich pastures are home to the cows that help produce Brie.

Burgundy brings dishes such as Boeuf Bourguignon and Coq au Vin instantly to mind. We also have this province to thank for escargots, Dijon mustard and cassis, a blackcurrant liqueur, as well as for some of the finest wines anyone could hope to sample.

Franche-Comté is a mountainous region that abounds with game and ways of preparing it, while mountain streams provide delicious trout.

Bordeaux, like Burgundy, is known for its fine wines. It is also the place of origin for two well-known brandies – Cognac and Armagnac. Another famous product of the region is the truffle, which grows wild in the forests. Pâtés and terrines seem almost to have been invented with truffles in mind and the area boasts many delicious pâté recipes.

In the south lie Languedoc, Roussillon and, of course, Provence, the food of these provinces reflecting all the color and warmth of the region. Languedoc has made cassoulets, casseroles of duck, pork or lamb with sausages and haricot beans, an important part of French cuisine. In Roussillon, the Spanish influence is strong and recipes use peppers and tomatoes freely. The flavor of Provence is one of herbs and garlic, sun-ripened tomatoes and good olive oil.

Each region in France has made its own important contribution to the national cuisine, so much so that it would be impossible to leave any one of them out. It is this wonderful combination of different tastes and styles of cooking that make us think of the pleasures of the table whenever we think of France.

CREAM OF TOMATO SOUP

*A rich and warming soup, ideal
for cold winter evenings.*

Step 2

Step 2

Step 2

☐ 4½ lbs tomatoes, quartered   ☐ 1 onion, finely chopped
☐ 8 cups chicken stock   ☐ 1 clove garlic, halved
☐ 1 sprig parsley, washed   ☐ 1 bay leaf   ☐ Pinch of thyme
☐ 2 tbsps olive oil   ☐ Salt and pepper   ☐ Few drops Tabasco

1. Warm the olive oil in a frying pan and gently cook the tomatoes and onions until very soft.

2. Transfer to a large saucepan and add the parsley, garlic, thyme, bay leaf, salt and pepper. Then add the stock. Bring to the boil, stirring well, then reduce the heat and simmer gently for 1½ hours.

3. Allow the soup to cool, then remove the bay leaf and blend the soup in an electric blender until smooth.

4. Reheat before serving, adding a few drops of Tabasco.

TIME   Allow 5 minutes preparation time, and at least 2 hours for cooking.

SERVING IDEAS   Decorate the soup by swirling through a little light cream.

VARIATION   Sprinkle over a few tablespoons of chopped fresh herbs, such as basil.

COOK'S TIP   The tomatoes can be seeded if preferred, although after blending the difference is negligible.

☐

OPPOSITE

CREAM OF
TOMATO SOUP

———— SERVES 4-6 ————

LEEK AND POTATO SOUP

*An economical, tasty soup that
is quick and easy to prepare.*

☐ 4 large leeks, thinly sliced ☐ 4 large potatoes, peeled and diced ☐ 4 cups chicken stock ☐ 2 cups water ☐ Salt and pepper ☐ 2 tbsps butter ☐ 4 tbsps heavy cream

TO SERVE

☐ 4 tbsps light cream ☐ 2 tbsps butter ☐ 1 tbsp fresh chopped parsley ☐ 1 tbsp fresh chopped chives

1. Melt 2 tbsps butter in a frying pan and gently cook the leeks. Do not allow them to brown too much. Remove from the heat.

2. Transfer the leeks to a large saucepan, add the potatoes, stock, water, salt and pepper, bring to the boil, cover and reduce heat. Simmer for approximately 35 minutes.

3. Add the potatoes for the last 20 minutes of cooking.

4. Once cooked, stir in the heavy cream.

5. Either serve the soup as it is, or blend until smooth in a blender or food processor.

6. Serve in a large soup tureen, with the remaining butter dotted over and the light cream swirled over the top. Sprinkle over the herbs at the last minute.

TIME   Preparation of the vegetables takes about 10 minutes, cooking time is approximately 45 minutes and final touches take about 5 minutes.

VARIATION   Instead of leeks use a different vegetable, such as spinach or watercress.

SERVING IDEAS   To make the soup richer, add a few tablespoons of milk when stiring in the heavy cream.

☐

OPPOSITE

LEEK AND
POTATO SOUP

—— SERVES 4 ——

AVOCADO PEARS
WITH CRAB

Serve this delicately-flavored appetizer
before a fish course; its success is assured.

Step 2

Step 5

☐ 2 avocados　☐ 1 small can crab meat
☐ 1 green pepper, seeded and pith removed
☐ 1 egg yolk, beaten　☐ ¾ cup oil (corn or similar)
☐ 1 tsp mustard　☐ 2 tbsps tomato ketchup
☐ 1 drop Tabasco　☐ 3 tbsps brandy
☐ Juice of 1 lemon　☐ Salt and pepper

1. Begin by making the cocktail sauce. Beat together the egg yolk, mustard, salt, pepper, tomato ketchup, Tabasco and brandy. Then add the oil, drop by drop, beating continuously.

2. Peel the avocados and cut them in half. Remove the stone and coat the flesh with the lemon juice to prevent discoloration.

3. Cut the pepper into thin matchsticks.

4. Drain the crab meat.

5. Slice the avocados thinly and evenly and mix them with the pepper matchsticks. Arrange neatly on a serving plate.

6. Sprinkle over the crab meat and coat with the cocktail sauce.

TIME　　Preparation takes approximately 25 minutes.

WATCHPOINT　　Do not cut the avocados too far in advance as they may discolor even with the coating of lemon juice.

VARIATION　　Use fresh crab if time and budget permit.

☐

OPPOSITE

AVOCADO PEARS
WITH CRAB

SERVES 6

ANCHOYADE

*This is an anchovy paste to spread on toast
and serve with a salad for a light meal.*

Step 3

□ 15 salted anchovy fillets   □ 2 cloves garlic, peeled
□ ½ cup olive oil   □ Few drops lemon juice

TO SERVE

□ 1 prepared lettuce   □ 4 tbsps vinaigrette sauce
□ 12 slices bread, toasted

1. Toss the lettuce in the vinaigrette sauce.

2. Rinse the anchovy fillets under cold running water to remove the excess salt. Pat them dry on kitchen paper.

3. Pound the garlic with a pestle and mortar until smooth.

4. Pound the fillets into the garlic until smooth.

5. Beat in the oil, a little at a time, until a smooth paste is formed.

6. Spread the mixture onto the slices of toast and place them on top of the tossed lettuce.

TIME   Preparation takes about 25 minutes.

VARIATION   The number of garlic cloves can be increased or decreased according to taste.

COOK'S TIP   Rinse the fillets very well. If they are extremely salty, soak for 1 hour in cold water before use.

PREPARATION   The anchoyade can be made in a blender – just put all the ingredients in together and blend until smooth.

Step 5

□

OPPOSITE

ANCHOYADE

--------- SERVES 4 ---------

HADDOCK MOUSSE

*A delicious, light mousse, delicately
flavored by the smoked haddock.*

Step 7

Step 7

Step 8

☐ 3 smoked haddock fillets ☐ ¾ cup heavy cream
☐ 1 cup fish stock ☐ 1 tbsp fresh chives, chopped
☐ 3 sheets gelatin ☐ Salt and pepper

1. Soak the gelatin in a bowl of cold water.

2. Cut one of the fillets in half and chop it finely. Use either a very sharp knife or a food processor.

3. In a saucepan, gently heat the fish stock and the chopped haddock fillet. Drain the gelatin sheets and stir into the stock until they have completely dissolved. Remove from the heat, transfer to a clean bowl and put in the refrigerator.

4. Meanwhile, whip the cream until it becomes light and fluffy. Keep cool.

5. Once the stock is completely cool, gently fold in the whipped cream, chives, salt and pepper.

6. Return mixture to the refrigerator for at least 2 hours.

7. Cut the remaining fillets into very thin slices and spread them out onto plastic wrap. Place spoonfuls of mousse down the center of each. There should be some mousse left over.

8. Using the plastic wrap to help you, gently roll up the slices of haddock to make a neat roll.

9. Put the rolls back into the refrigerator until ready to serve.

10. Using a teaspoon, form the remaining mousse into small oblong shapes, and serve with the haddock roll. Remove the plastic wrap before serving.

TIME   It will take approximately 1 hour to prepare the haddock mousse and 2 hours for it to set.

VARIATION   Use different herbs in the mousse to give alternative subtle flavors.

SERVING IDEAS   Serve a light dressing with the haddock, such as a blend of olive oil, lemon juice and a little salt and pepper.

☐

OPPOSITE

HADDOCK
MOUSSE

SERVES 6

PEASANT'S SOUP

*A hearty vegetable soup, with a little bacon for
added flavor; great for meals on cold days.*

Step 4

☐ 4 cups chicken stock   ☐ 1½ cups leeks, chopped
☐ 2 cups potatoes, peeled and diced
☐ 1 cup cabbage, shredded
☐ 1 turnip, diced   ☐ ½ cup smoked bacon, chopped
☐ 2 tbsps goose or other poultry drippings
☐ Salt and pepper

TO SERVE

☐ 4 slices of bread   ☐ 1 cup Cheddar cheese, grated

1. Blanch the cabbage in boiling salted water. Drain well.

2. Shred the cabbage into a large saucepan and set aside.

3. In another saucepan, fry the bacon in the dripping and stir in all the vegetables except the potatoes.

4. Pour the stock over the shredded cabbage and bring to the boil. Transfer the bacon and vegetable mixture into the cabbage and stock. Season with salt and pepper.

5. Bring to the boil once again, cover, reduce the heat and simmer very gently for approximately 1½ hours.

6. Add the potato for the last 20 minutes of cooking. Check the level of the liquid during cooking; if it should get too low add a little water.

7. Sprinkle the cheese over the bread, and toast under a broiler. Cut into small triangles or rounds and serve on a small plate with the soup.

TIME   Preparation takes about 15 minutes, and cooking takes about 1 hour and 50 minutes.

SERVING IDEA   Ladle the soup into individual bowls once it is cooked. Float the bread with the cheese sprinkled over on the top and brown under a broiler.

WATCHPOINT   Check the liquid level carefully, adding water as necessary.

PREPARATION   Choose a good, fresh green cabbage for this simple but delicious soup.

☐

OPPOSITE

PEASANT'S SOUP

—— SERVES 4 ——

COCKLE RAVIOLI

A highly original dish, ideal as an appetizer for an intimate dinner party.

Step 6

□ 2 ¼ lbs cockles   □ ½ clove garlic, crushed
□ 4 tbsps fresh parsley (discard the stalk and just snip off the ends)
□ 2 cups all-purpose flour   □ 2 eggs   □ Salt
□ ½ cup light cream   □ 1 cup white wine   □ 2 tbsps butter
□ 4 sprigs parsley   □ 1 extra egg, beaten

1. Make the ravioli dough by mixing the flour, 2 eggs and a little salt together. Form into a ball and put in the refrigerator.

2. Place the wine and the cockles in a frying pan over a high heat to open the shells. Once the shells are open, remove the pan from the heat and take out the shells. Cut away the tail part of the cockle and strain the liquor through a fine sieve or cheesecloth.

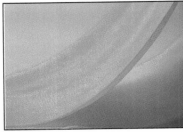
Step 6

3. In a clean frying pan, sauté the cockles in the butter with the chopped parsley and the garlic.

4. Blanch the parsley sprigs in boiling water. Drain well. In a blender, blend the parsley and the drained liquor together until smooth. Transfer to a saucepan and reduce by ¾ over a high heat.

5. Once reduced, stir in the cream, bring to the boil, work once again in the blender and strain through a cheesecloth. Keep warm.

Step 7

6. Roll the ravioli dough very thin on a lightly-floured surface or, if you have a pasta press, pass it through the thinnest press possible. Cut dough into the desired shape.

7. Place a few cockles in the center and either fold up the dough or place another piece of dough on top. Brush the edges well with the beaten egg and pinch edges together with thumb and forefinger to seal well. Coat both sides of the ravioli with a little beaten egg.

Step 7

8. Set a large quantity of water to boil, add 1 tsp salt and cook the ravioli for 3 minutes (a little longer if you prefer your pasta well cooked). Drain well. Serve hot with the sauce poured over.

TIME   Preparation takes about 20 minutes and cooking takes about 1 hour and 20 minutes in all.

VARIATION   Any type of small seafood can be used instead of the cockles.

WATCHPOINT   Do not forget to brush the edges of the dough shapes well with the beaten egg. If joining two pieces together, brush the edges of both pieces.

□

OPPOSITE

COCKLE RAVIOLI

—— SERVES 4 ——

SNAILS WITH POTATOES
IN NUTMEG

*This completely new way of serving snails will provide
a great dish to delight guests at your next dinner party.*

Step 2

Step 2

Step 3

□ 8 medium-sized potatoes
□ 40 canned snails, cooked and rinsed,   □ 1½ cups light cream
□ Freshly ground nutmeg   □ Salt and pepper

1. Peel the potatoes and cut them into regular-sized slices. Blanch them for 30 seconds in lightly salted boiling water, then drain well.

2. Place the potatoes in a frying pan, add the cream, nutmeg to taste, salt and pepper.

3. Add the snails and cook over a gentle heat until the potatoes are quite tender.

4. Once the potatoes are cooked, arrange them in a rose pattern with the snails in the middle and the cream sauce poured over.

TIME   Preparation takes about 5 minutes and cooking takes about 40 minutes.

SERVING IDEAS   Sprinkle over a little chopped red or green basil.

WATCHPOINT   The dish is ready to serve as soon as the potatoes are cooked.

©Copyright F. Lebain

□

OPPOSITE

SNAILS WITH
POTATOES IN
NUTMEG

SERVES 8

PISTOU SOUP

A nourishing vegetable soup served with fresh basil and garlic sauce.

□ 1½ cups lima beans, pre-soaked overnight
□ 1 large potato, peeled and diced   □ 2 carrots, diced
2 zucchini, diced   □ 1 stick celery, wiped and diced
□ 3 cups green beans   □ 2 leeks, white parts only, finely sliced
□ 1 large onion, finely sliced
□ 5 tomatoes, seeded and chopped   □ 8 cups chicken stock
□ 6 cloves garlic   □ 1 bouquet garni   □ Salt and pepper
□ 2 cloves garlic   □ 35 fresh basil leaves, wiped
□ ½ cup olive oil

1. Rinse the soaked beans and cook them for approximately 1 hour in lightly salted boiling water, until tender. Drain well and keep warm.

2. Warm 4 tbsps olive oil and 4 tbsps water in a large saucepan and cook all the vegetables, except the potato, tomato and garlic, over a high heat for 10 minutes. Shake the saucepan to prevent sticking.

3. Pour over the stock, add the bouquet garni and season with salt and pepper. Bring to the boil, reduce the heat, cover and simmer for 30 to 40 minutes.

4. Add the potato for the last 15 minutes of cooking.

5. To make the Pistou sauce, pound the garlic, basil leaves and tomato together in a pestle and mortar. Slowly beat in the oil, a little at a time, beating continuously until the mixture is smooth. The sauce can be made in a blender if preferred. Season with salt and pepper.

6. Five minutes before serving the soup, stir in the beans. Serve the soup in a large tureen, passing the sauce in a separate bowl for guests to help themselves.

TIME   Preparation takes about 40 minutes and cooking takes approximately 2 hours.

SERVING IDEAS   Serve with garlic-flavored toasted croutons.

VARIATION   The Pistou sauce can be stirred into the soup in the tureen before serving.

□

OPPOSITE

PISTOU SOUP

---- SERVES 6 ----

CAULIFLOWER AND PARSLEY CREAM

Rich and creamy, this soup is a magical blend
of cauliflower and parsley.

Step 4

Step 4

- □ 1lb cauliflower, washed and chopped
- □ 1½ cups leeks, white part only, cut into thin slices
- □ 4 cups chicken stock   □ 5 tbsps flat-leaved parsley, washed
- □ ½ cup heavy cream   □ ¼ cup butter

1. Melt half of the butter in a frying pan and cook the leeks until tender. Add the stock and the cauliflower.

2. Stir well and bring to the boil. Reduce the heat and simmer gently for 35 minutes. Retain ½ cup of the soup for Step 4.

3. Blend the remainder of the soup with a hand mixer until smooth. Stir in the cream and the remaining butter, season well and set aside.

4. Blanch the parsley in salted boiling water, drain well and then, adding 2 tbsps of the cauliflower soup, blend with a hand mixer until smooth.

5. Serve the rest of the cauliflower soup in individual bowls, swirling the blended parsley over.

TIME   Preparation takes about 15 minutes and cooking takes approximately 50 minutes.

COOK'S TIP   The soup can be made in advance, kept in the refrigerator and reheated just before serving.

WATCHPOINT   The soup should be removed from the heat as soon as the cauliflower is cooked through in Step 2. Do not overcook; the 35 minutes mentioned is just an indication.

□

OPPOSITE

CAULIFLOWER AND
PARSLEY CREAM

—— SERVES 6 ——

PUMPKIN SOUP

*An unusual blend of sweet and sour flavors
go together to make a lovely soup.*

Step 1

Step 3

☐ 3 lbs pumpkin, peeled and cut into cubes   ☐ 1 cup milk
☐ 1 cup heavy cream   ☐ 1 tsp cinnamon   ☐ Salt and pepper

1. Cook the pumpkin in boiling salted water until tender; approximately 20 minutes. Drain well.

2. Mash the pumpkin with a fork, stir in the milk, return to the heat and bring to the boil.

3. Blend with a hand mixer or in a blender until smooth.

4. Reheat, remove from the heat, stir in the cream and cinnamon, and season well. Serve hot.

TIME   Preparation takes about 10 minutes, and cooking takes approximately 40 minutes.

WATCHPOINT   Make sure that you drain the pumpkin well, otherwise the soup will be too thin.

SERVING IDEAS   Decorate the soup by swirling over a few spoonfuls of light cream and sprinkling with chopped chives.

VARIATION   1 cup of grated Cheddar cheese added before reheating at Step 4 gives a pleasant flavor.

☐

OPPOSITE

PUMPKIN SOUP

—— SERVES 6 ——

ONION SOUP

*Traditionally consumed in the early hours after a night
out on the town, this is a hearty, nourishing soup.*

Step 1

☐ ½ cup butter   ☐ 6 large onions, sliced   ☐ Salt and pepper
☐ 4 cups chicken stock   ☐ 4 slices bread, toasted
☐ 2 cloves garlic, crushed   ☐ 1 cup grated cheese
☐ ½ cup white wine

1. In a large saucepan, melt the butter and cook the onion and garlic gently for approximately 30 minutes, stirring from time to time to prevent sticking. Add salt and pepper.

2. Remove from heat, stir in the wine and stock, return to the heat and bring to the boil, stirring continuously. Reduce heat and simmer for 30 minutes. If the soup appears too thick, stir in a little water.

3. Serve the soup in individual bowls. Cut the toast into cubes. Place the cubes on the soup, sprinkle over the grated cheese and place under a hot broiler for a few minutes to melt the cheese.

TIME   Preparation takes 15 minutes and cooking takes 1 hour. To brown the top, an additional 5 minutes will be needed.

PREPARATION   Rub a clove of garlic over the toast before you cut it into cubes.

COOK'S TIP   If you do not have a broiler, put the bowls into a very hot oven for a few minutes.

VARIATION   Red wine can be used instead of white, if desired.

☐

OPPOSITE

ONION SOUP

—— SERVES 4 ——

HERBY GOAT CHEESE

*Fresh goat's cheese is very popular in France, and
is becoming more popular in other parts of the
world. Its sometimes bland flavor is enlivened
by the addition of herbs in this recipe.*

□ 2 fresh goat cheeses   □ Few drops lemon juice
□ Few drops vinegar   □ ½ tsp olive oil   □ 10 capers
□ 5 peppercorns
□ 1 tbsp mixed fresh herbs, such as chives, parsley and chervil
□ 1 tbsp finely chopped onion and shallot   □ Salt and pepper

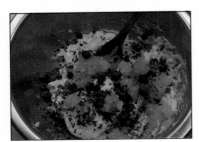

Step 2

Step 3

1. Mix the cheeses with the chopped herbs, onion and shallot.

2. Mix in the capers, peppercorns and the salt and pepper.

3. Stir in the vinegar, lemon juice and olive oil. Stir well.

4. Place the cheese into 4 small custard cups, pushing it down
well, and then set in the refrigerator for approximately 2 hours.

5. Turn out just before serving.

TIME   Preparation takes about 40 minutes.

SERVING IDEAS   Serve with a mixed salad tossed in vinaigrette
sauce.

COOK'S TIP   Use only fresh goat cheese; avoid the dry variety
which is often available, as it will crumble and will not mix in well.

□

OPPOSITE

HERBY GOAT
CHEESE

OMELETTES GOURMANDES

*Lovely, rich-tasting omelets, these are
perfect for a quick evening meal.*

Step 3

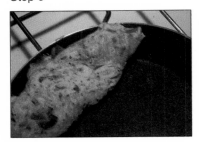

Step 4

☐ 12 eggs, beaten   ☐ 4 onions, finely chopped
☐ 1 tbsp fresh herbs, chopped   ☐ 1 cup mushrooms, sliced
☐ 5 tbsps oil   ☐ Salt and pepper

---

1. Sauté the onions in 2 tablespoons of oil over a high heat, then reduce the heat and cook for a further 20 minutes.

2. In another frying pan, sauté the mushrooms in 1 tablespoon of oil. Remove from the heat.

3. Add the beaten eggs to the mushrooms, stir in half of the onions, and cook over a high heat in as much of the remaining oil as necessary. Sprinkle over the herbs and cook the omelet until the base is crisp but the filling is still slightly liquid.

4. Fold one side of the omelet into the middle, then fold over the other side.

5. Serve on a bed of the remaining onions with a little salt and pepper.

TIME   It takes about 8 minutes to prepare the omelet and 8-10 minutes to cook it. Cooking time for the onions is about 20 minutes.

WATCHPOINT   Take care not to overcook the omelet; it should be served a little liquid in the center.

SERVING IDEAS   Sprinkle a little diced red pepper around the edges of the omelet.

VARIATION   A multitude of ingredients can be added to omelets; try chopped chicken livers, for example.

☐

OPPOSITE

OMELETTES
GOURMANDES

— SERVES 4 —

SCRAMBLED EGGS
WITH OLIVES

*The addition of black olives to scrambled eggs
turns this simple dish into a memorable one.*

Step 1

Step 4

Step 5

☐ 12 eggs   ☐ 4 tomatoes, seeded and chopped
☐ 15 black olives, stoned   ☐ 1 clove garlic, chopped
☐ ½ cup olive oil   ☐ 1 small onion, chopped
☐ 2 tbsps butter   ☐ Salt and pepper

1. Beat the eggs and set them aside.

2. Mince the tomatoes and the olives together finely using a food processor or mixer.

3. Warm the olive oil in a frying pan, increase the heat to high and cook the onion, garlic, tomatoes and olives until all the juices have evaporated.

4. Cook the eggs in the butter over a gentle heat, stirring continuously with a wooden spoon.

5. Once the eggs are cooked, stir in the tomato/olive mixture.

6. Serve on small, pre-warmed plates.

TIME   Preparation takes about 30 minutes and cooking takes 30 minutes.

SERVING IDEAS   Delicious with hot toast or muffins. Serve with salad and a fresh French stick for a light meal.

☐

OPPOSITE

SCRAMBLED EGGS
WITH OLIVES

QUICHE LORRAINE

Originally from the Lorraine region of France,
this pie recipe is now famed world-wide.

Step 1

Step 2

DOUGH

☐ 1½ cups all-purpose flour   ☐ ⅜ cup butter   ☐ Pinch of salt
☐ ½ egg beaten with 1 tbsp water

FILLING

☐ 3 thick strips bacon, diced   ☐ ½ cup all-purpose flour, sieved
☐ 4 eggs, beaten   ☐ ¾ cup heavy cream   ☐ ⅓ cup milk
☐ Pinch grated nutmeg   ☐ Salt and pepper

1. To make the dough, rub the butter into the flour with your fingertips until the mixture resembles fine breadcrumbs. Add the salt and bind the mixture together with the beaten egg and a little cold water. Put into the fridge for 5 minutes to rest.

2. Preheat the oven to 375°F. Roll out the pastry to the size of the pie dish and, being careful not to stretch or tear the dough, line the pie dish.

3. Dot the base of the pie with the diced bacon.

4. Beat together the eggs, flour, milk, cream, nutmeg and a little salt and pepper.

5. Pour the egg mixture into the flan and cook immediately in the oven for approximately 35 to 40 minutes.

TIME   Preparation takes about 30 minutes and cooking takes 40 minutes.

PREPARATION   The dough can be made in advance and kept in the fridge.

COOK'S TIP   The pie case can be prepared a day in advance and baked blind for 15 minutes.

VARIATION   Add a handful of grated cheese to the egg mixture.

SERVING IDEAS   Make small individual pies instead of one large one, reducing cooking time by 5 minutes.

☐

OPPOSITE

QUICHE LORRAINE

—————— SERVES 6 ——————

CHEESE SOUFFLE

*This puffy, golden souffle will delight your
guests, but rush it to the table immediately
on removal from the oven!*

Step 2

Step 2

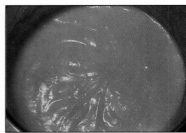
Step 3

☐ 2 tbsps butter   ☐ 1½ cups grated cheese
☐ ¼ cup all-purpose flour   ☐ 1 cup milk   ☐ Pinch of nutmeg
☐ 4 eggs, separated   ☐ 1 extra egg white   ☐ Butter for greasing
☐ Salt and pepper

1. Preheat the oven to 375°F. Grease a souffle dish with butter
and sprinkle inside 3 tbsps of the grated cheese.

2. Melt the butter in a heavy saucepan, whisk in the flour, cook
for about a minute, pour in all the milk and whisk continuously
until the mixture thickens. Reduce the heat and cook for 2
minutes.

3. Add the salt, pepper, nutmeg and the egg yolks one by one,
beating well with a wooden spoon. Leave to cool for about 5
minutes.

4. Stir the remaining cheese into the white sauce. Whisk the 5 egg
whites until firm. Fold them gently into the cheese mixture with a
metal spoon.

5. Pour the mixture into the prepared souffle dish and cook in the
oven for 40-45 minutes.

6. The souffle should be well risen and golden-topped. Serve
immediately.

TIME   Preparation takes approximately 20 minutes, and
cooking takes 40-45 minutes.

SERVING IDEAS   At Step 5 the mixture could be poured into 6
individual buttered and "cheesed" custard cups. Cooking time
will be reduced to 20-25 minutes.

VARIATION   ¼ cup crumbled blue cheese gives an unusual,
but pleasant, flavor.

☐

OPPOSITE

CHEESE SOUFFLE

—— SERVES 6 ——

CHICKEN AND WALNUT SALAD

Walnuts add a refined flavor to this chicken and cheese salad.

☐ 1lb cooked chicken breast   ☐ Juice of 1 lemon
☐ ¾ cup shelled walnuts   ☐ 2 cups prepared mixed salad
☐ 6 oz Emmenthal cheese   ☐ 1 green apple, diced
☐ 1 red apple, diced

SAUCE

☐ ½ cup yogurt   ☐ 1 tbsp mustard   ☐ ½ cup olive oil
☐ 2 tbsps wine vinegar   ☐ 2 tbsps ground walnuts
☐ Salt and pepper

Step 4

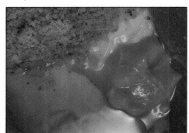

Step 4

Step 4

1. Pour the lemon juice over the apples as soon as they have been diced to prevent them from discoloring. Toss well to coat.

2. Cut the chicken breasts into neat cubes and mix with the apple and shelled walnuts.

3. Cut the cheese into neat cubes and add to the above.

4. Mix the ingredients for the sauce together in a bowl or screw-top jar, shake well and pour the sauce over the chicken and apple mixture.

5. Place a little salad on each of 6 small plates, add the chicken mixture and serve.

TIME   Preparation takes about 30 minutes.

SLIMMER'S TIP   Use a diet yogurt and leave out the olive oil.

VARIATION   If Emmenthal is not available, use Cheddar.

COOK'S TIP   Grind the walnuts as finely as possible to allow their flavor to develop fully.

☐

OPPOSITE

CHICKEN AND
WALNUT SALAD

SERVES 6

STUFFED ARTICHOKE HEARTS

A very popular vegetable in France, the artichoke is put to excellent use in this recipe.

Step 1

Step 1

□ 6 large artichoke hearts (freshly cooked or canned)
□ ½ cup ground ham
□ ½ cup ground Parma ham, or similar smoked ham
□ 1 cup mushrooms, rinsed, wiped and finely chopped
□ 1 cup grated cheese   □ Juice of 1 lemon   □ Nut butter
□ Salt and pepper

SAUCE

□ 1 cup milk   □ ¼ cup all-purpose flour   □ 2 tbsps butter
□ 3 tbsps light cream   □ Pinch nutmeg   □ Salt and pepper

1. Cook the artichoke hearts in boiling water with the juice of ½ the lemon until tender. Drain well and remove the 'beard'. Coat with the remaining lemon juice. Set aside.

2. Cook the mushrooms in the nut of butter over a high heat for a few minutes, until their juices run. Remove from the heat and discard the juices.

3. Stir the ham, salt and pepper into the mushrooms and heat through completely.

4. To make the sauce, melt the butter, beat in the flour, and cook for 1 minute. Pour in all the milk and beat continuously until the mixture thickens. Reduce the heat and cook for a further 2 minutes. Remove from heat and stir in the nutmeg, salt and cream.

5. Stir ¾ of the cheese into the ham and mushroom mixture. Pile this mixture onto the artichoke hearts.

6. Grease an ovenproof dish, place the prepared artichokes in it, spoon the sauce over each artichoke and sprinkle over the remaining grated cheese.

7. Cook in a hot oven for 10-15 minutes, until hot and well browned on the top.

TIME   Preparation takes about 25 minutes and total cooking time is about 35 minutes.

WATCHPOINT   Ensure that the artichoke is well covered with the lemon juice to prevent discoloration.

SERVING IDEAS   If time permits, pour the sauce neatly over each individual artichoke, then sprinkle over the cheese and continue cooking as above.

BUYING GUIDE   Use the large variety of artichoke sometimes called Brittany artichoke.

□

OPPOSITE

STUFFED
ARTICHOKE
HEARTS

SERVES 5-6

CHICKEN LIVER SALAD

A smooth blend of chicken livers and artichoke hearts produces this tasty salad.

Step 1

Step 1

Step 1

□ 12 chicken livers   □ 1lb mixed salad   □ 2 large artichokes
□ 1 nut butter   □ 3 cups oil (peanut or similar)
□ 1 tbsp wine vinegar   □ 1 small onion, finely chopped
□ Juice of 1 lemon   □ Salt and pepper

1. Prepare the artichokes by removing the hard end and then cutting off all the outer leaves with a small, sharp knife.

2. Cook the artichokes in salted boiling water into which you have poured the lemon juice. Cooking time is approximately 15 to 20 minutes.

3. Melt the butter in a frying pan, add 2 tbsps oil and cook the liver and onion over a moderately-high heat for about 5 minutes. Deglaze the pan with 1 tbsp vinegar, reduce the heat and cook for a further 4 to 5 minutes.

4. Arrange the liver, followed by the artichoke, on a bed of salad on small individual plates.

5. Warm the remaining vinegar and mix in the oil, a little salt and freshly-ground pepper. Pour a little of this sauce over each individual salad.

TIME   Preparation takes approximately 30 minutes and cooking takes about 20 minutes.

VARIATION   Watercress gives a very pleasant taste to this salad. Make sure it has been rinsed in plenty of cold running water and that any hard stalks have been discarded.

□

OPPOSITE

CHICKEN
LIVER SALAD

—— SERVES 6 ——

SAUERKRAUT SALAD

*A salad from the Alsace region, where the German
influence in the cooking is unmistakable.*

Step 2

Step 2

☐ 3 ½ cups cooked, fresh sauerkraut, pre-soaked for 2 hours in
cold water   ☐ 2 carrots, grated   ☐ 5 tbsps olive oil
☐ 2 tbsps wine vinegar   ☐ 1 red apple, diced
☐ 2 small onions, chopped   ☐ 1 tsp sugar   ☐ 1 tsp cinnamon
☐ ½ tsp salt   ☐ Pepper   ☐ Juice of 1 lemon

1. In a large salad bowl, mix together the oil, vinegar, sugar,
pepper, cinnamon and salt until all the sugar and salt has
dissolved.

2. Wash the sauerkraut in cold water and drain well. Remove any
excess moisture with a dry tea towel. Cut the dry sauerkraut into
even lengths.

3. Pour the lemon juice over the apple, onion and carrot.

4. Mix all the ingredients together in the salad bowl, turning well
to incorporate the sauce.

TIME   Pre-soak the sauerkraut for at least 2 hours. It takes
about 20 minutes to prepare this salad.

SERVING IDEAS   In Alsace this salad is often served with slices
of sweetbread sausage.

VARIATION   Add a little German sausage or liver sausage, cut
into small cubes.

WATCHPOINT   Make sure the apple is well coated with the
lemon juice to prevent discoloration.

PREPARATION   This salad can be made in advance and kept in
the fridge, but add the diced apple just before serving.

☐

OPPOSITE

SAUERKRAUT
SALAD

SERVES 6

FISHERMAN'S SALAD

A new dish to serve as an elegant appetizer to any meal. Care must be taken in the preparation of the vegetables, but the stunning result makes it well worth the effort.

Step 1

Step 1

Step 1

□ 1 carrot, scraped   □ ½ cucumber, wiped, peeled and seeded
□ 1 red pepper, seeded   □ 1 zucchini, wiped
□ About 40 small shrimp, peeled (retain peelings)
□ 1 tbsp olive oil   □ 1 tbsp brandy or cognac
□ ⅔ cup light cream   □ Juice of ½ lemon
□ 2 tbsps fresh chervil, chopped

1. Cut each of the vegetables carefully into thin strips. As you finish each vegetable, put the strips in the fridge to keep them crisp and fresh.

2. Fry the shrimp peelings briskly over a high heat for 5 minutes in the olive oil. Add the brandy or cognac and flambé the mixture. Allow the alcohol to burn out, then stir in the cream, and continue cooking over a low heat for about 10 minutes.

3. Strain the sauce through a fine sieve, discarding all but the smooth sauce. Blend the sauce with a hand mixer and then put the sauce in the fridge to cool.

4. On a serving dish, spread a single bed of the vegetable strips and sprinkle over the peeled shrimp.

5. Add the lemon juice to the cooled sauce, stir well and pour it over the salad. Sprinkle over the chervil and serve.

TIME   Preparation takes about 35 minutes.

COOK'S TIP   The sauce can be made in advance and kept in the fridge.

PREPARATION   Vegetables can be prepared on the morning of serving the dish, and kept covered in the fridge.

□

OPPOSITE

FISHERMAN'S
SALAD

—— SERVES 8 ——

BUTTERED CABBAGE

*A great way of serving the humble cabbage. The
addition of bacon and onion adds a delicious flavor.*

Step 1

Step 1

☐ 3 ¼ lbs cabbage, shredded   ☐ ½ lb smoked bacon, chopped
☐ ½ cup onion, chopped
☐ ½ cup goose or other poultry dripping or lard
☐ ½ cup butter   ☐ Salt and pepper

1. Blanch the cabbage in boiling salted water. Drain well.

2. Melt the dripping or lard in a large frying pan. Add the bacon,
onion and cabbage, and stir well.

3. Cover and cook over a very gentle heat for 20 minutes.

4. Stir in the butter and cook for a further 20 minutes, covered.

5. Serve on a pre-heated serving dish.

TIME   Preparation takes about 10 minutes and cooking takes
about 45 minutes

WATCHPOINT   Ensure that the cabbage is well drained after
blanching.

COOK'S TIP   Do not use the outer leaves of the cabbage as
they are usually hard and bitter.

☐

OPPOSITE

BUTTERED
CABBAGE

SERVES 6

FRICASSEE DE CAROTTES

Sautéed carrots, gently cooked with onions and smoked bacon.

Step 1

Step 3

☐ 3 ⅓ lbs carrots, peeled and finely sliced into rounds
☐ 1lb onions, finely sliced ☐ 1 bouquet garni
☐ 3 tbsps goose or poultry dripping
☐ ¾ lb smoked bacon, diced
☐ 1 tsp sugar ☐ ½ tsp cinnamon ☐ Salt and pepper

1. In a large, heavy-based frying pan, gently melt the goose or poultry dripping, increase the heat and sauté the carrots, onions and bouquet garni.

2. Shake the pan from time to time to prevent sticking. Once the vegetables begin to color, reduce the heat, cover and cook for 25-30 minutes.

3. Blanch the bacon in boiling water, drain well and add to the carrot mixture.

4. Sprinkle over the sugar and cinnamon, cover and continue to cook until very tender.

TIME   Preparation takes about 25 minutes and cooking takes approximately 1 hour.

SERVING IDEAS   Sprinkle over a little chopped chives or parsley.

WATCHPOINT   Cook the carrots very gently so that they do not dry out.

☐

OPPOSITE

FRICASSEE DE
CAROTTES

—— SERVES 6 ——

CHICKEN BREAST SALAD

*An eye-catching presentation of tomato, avocado,
lettuce and golden chicken breast, this salad
is a filling appetizer for a light main course.*

☐ 3 chicken breasts   ☐ 2 avocados, peeled, stoned and sliced,
with the juice of 1 lemon poured over
☐ 2 cups mixed lettuce, washed, dried and chopped
☐ ⅔ cup white wine   ☐ ⅓ cup heavy cream
☐ ¾ cup chicken stock   ☐ 4 tomatoes   ☐ 1 nut butter
☐ Salt and pepper

1. Melt the butter in a frying pan and quickly seal the chicken on all sides. Deglaze the frying pan with the white wine, pour over the stock and cook over a moderate heat until the stock reduces by half.

2. Reduce the heat to as low as possible, cover the pan and cook for a further 8 minutes. Remove from the heat.

3. Set the chicken breasts aside, return the pan to the heat, stir in the cream, and season with salt and pepper. Stir continuously until the sauce thickens somewhat.

4. Peel two of the tomatoes, seed them, cut them into thin sticks and then dice them.

5. Cut the remaining 2 tomatoes into thin slices.

6. Interlace the tomato slices and the avocado slices around a bed of lettuce. Place the sliced chicken breasts in the middle. Dot the diced tomato over and pour over the sauce.

Step 4

Step 4

TIME   Preparation takes about 30 minutes and cooking takes approximately 30 minutes.

VARIATION   Toss the lettuce in a little vinaigrette sauce before use.

WATCHPOINT   Coat the slices of avocado really well with the lemon juice to prevent too much discoloration.

Step 4

☐

OPPOSITE

CHICKEN
BREAST SALAD

SERVES 4

POMMES DARPHIN
AUX OIGNONS

*Decorative and tasty, these potato patties will
be appreciated by all. Serve with the Sunday roast
instead of the usual roast potatoes.*

Step 1

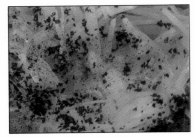

Step 2

Step 3

☐ 4 large potatoes, peeled   ☐ 1 onion, finely chopped
☐ 2 tbsps oil   ☐ 1 tbsp fresh herbs, chopped
☐ Salt and pepper

1. Cut the potatoes into small matchsticks, either by hand or in a machine.

2. Stir the onion and the herbs into the potato.

3. Oil 4 small molds and place the mixture evenly into each mold. Season each patty with salt and pepper.

4. Cook in a hot oven for 15 minutes, turning the patties over once halfway through the cooking time.

TIME   Preparation takes about 20 minutes and cooking takes 15 minutes.

VARIATION   Add a grated apple to the potato mixture.

COOK'S TIP   Press the potato mixture down well into the base of the molds.

☐

OPPOSITE

POMMES DARPHIN
AUX OIGNONS

BAKED EGGPLANT

*Cooked and served in small dishes, baked eggplant
makes a pleasant change from everyday vegetables.*

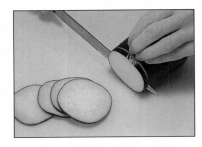

Step 1

Step 1

☐ 4 medium-sized eggplants, wiped and evenly sliced
☐ 2 ¼ lbs tomatoes, seeded and sliced ☐ 2 cloves garlic
☐ 1 bay leaf ☐ Pinch thyme ☐ 1 tbsp fresh parsley, chopped
☐ 1 cup grated cheese ☐ 6 tbsps olive oil ☐ Salt and pepper

1. Spread the eggplant slices out onto a serving plate and sprinkle liberally with salt. Allow to stand for about 30 minutes then wipe dry with paper towels. Fry the eggplant in 4 tbsps of the olive oil over a high heat, but take care not to let it burn.

2. Remove the slices from the frying pan and drain on paper towels. Retain any oil left in the pan.

3. Add the remaining olive oil and cook the garlic cloves gently so that they flavor the oil. Remove the cloves and discard. Add the tomatoes, bay leaf and thyme and cook for 20 minutes. Remove the bay leaf.

4. Pour half of this mixture into the base of an ovenproof dish, sprinkle over the parsley and add a little salt and pepper.

5. Lay the slices of eggplant over the above, followed by half of the cheese, then the rest of the tomato mixture and lastly the remaining cheese.

6. Cook in a hot oven for about 10 minutes, until nicely browned.

TIME   Preparation takes about 10 minutes and cooking takes about 40 minutes.

SERVING IDEAS   To make an attractive presentation, alternate layers of eggplant and tomato mixture in small dishes.

BUYING GUIDE   For best results buy medium-sized, shiny eggplant.

☐

OPPOSITE

BAKED EGGPLANT

—————— SERVES 4 ——————

LAMB SWEETBREAD SALAD

Step 1

Step 3

☐ ¾ lb lamb sweetbreads   ☐ 1 head lettuce, washed and dried
☐ 1 tsp fresh chervil, chopped   ☐ 1 tbsp flour
☐ 2 tbsps mayonnaise   ☐ 1 tbsp chicken stock
☐ 1 tsp Xeres vinegar, or good quality wine vinegar
☐ 1 tbsp butter   ☐ Salt and pepper

1. Blanch the sweetbreads in boiling water for 1 minute, and remove and discard the nerves. Chop the sweetbreads into bite-sized pieces, sprinkle over a little salt and pepper, and roll them in the flour.

2. Stir the vinegar into the mayonnaise, then stir in the stock – this should give a slightly thick sauce. Stir in the chervil and a little salt and pepper.

3. Sauté the sweetbreads in the butter, and drain when cooked.

4. Serve on a bed of lettuce leaves, with the chervil sauce poured over.

TIME   Preparation takes about 10 minutes and cooking takes 35 minutes.

VARIATION   Veal sweetbreads can be used instead of lamb, but these would need to be cut into small pieces prior to Step 3.

COOK'S TIP   After draining the sweetbreads, place them on paper towels to soak up any excess fat.

☐

OPPOSITE

LAMB
SWEETBREAD
SALAD

——— SERVES 4-6 ———

GRATIN DAUPHINOIS

*Cook this dish as slowly as possible and you will be
rewarded with a sumptuous, creamy delight.*

Step 1

☐ 4½ lbs potatoes, peeled and sliced   ☐ 2 cups light cream
☐ 1 clove garlic, peeled and crushed   ☐ 2 tbsps butter
☐ 1 cup grated cheese   ☐ Pinch nutmeg   ☐ Salt and pepper

1. Grease an ovenproof dish with the butter and spread the sliced potato into the base.

2. Mix the cream with the garlic, salt, pepper and nutmeg.

3. Pour the cream mixture over the potato and cook gently in a warm oven for 1½ hours, adding a little milk if the cream does not cover the potatoes.

4. Set the oven to its highest temperature, spinkle over the grated cheese and cook until crisp and golden brown.

TIME   Preparation takes about 10 minutes and cooking takes about 1 hour and 45 minutes.

VARIATION   A layer of thinly-sliced onion in the middle of the potatoes adds a distinctive flavor.

WATCHPOINT   The slow cooking of the dauphinois is very important. Do not be tempted to increase the temperature of the oven.

☐

OPPOSITE

GRATIN
DAUPHINOIS

—— SERVES 6 ——

BROCCOLI GRATIN

A typically French way of serving tasty broccoli.

Step 1

Step 1

□ 3 large heads broccoli, waste and hard ends removed
□ 2 tbsps butter   □ ¼ cup flour   □ 1 cup milk
□ 4 tbsps heavy cream   □ ¾ cup grated cheese
□ Pinch nutmeg   □ Salt and pepper

1. Cook the broccoli heads in salted boiling water until just underdone and slightly crisp. Plunge them immediately into cold water to stop them from cooking any further, and drain well.

2. Make the white sauce in a saucepan by melting the butter, whiping in the flour, cooking for one minute and then whipping in all the milk in one go. Whip continuously for 2 minutes.

3. Remove the sauce from the heat, and stir in the cream, nutmeg, salt, pepper and half of the cheese.

4. Chop the broccoli roughly with a sharp knife, mix with the sauce and pour into an ovenproof dish.

5. Sprinkle over the remaining cheese and cook in a hot oven until the top is crisp and brown – approximately 15 minutes.

COOK'S TIP   The flowerets of broccoli cook more quickly than the stalks, so separate the two and remove the flowerets a minute or two before the stalks.

TIME   Preparation takes about 10 minutes and cooking takes 55 minutes.

PREPARATION   Cook the broccoli in advance and store in the fridge.

ECONOMY   Make a large quantity of white sauce, pour into small containers and store in the freezer to use as necessary.

VARIATION   Use cauliflower if broccoli is not available.

□

OPPOSITE

BROCCOLI GRATIN

TURNIPS IN CREAM

*A marvelous recipe that transforms plain turnips
into a gourmet vegetable.*

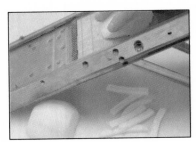

Step 1

Step 1

☐ 2 ¼ lbs turnips, peeled   ☐ ½ lb smoked bacon, diced
☐ 1 cup light cream   ☐ Pinch nutmeg   ☐ Salt and pepper

1. Cut the turnips into small cubes and blanch them for 2 minutes in lightly salted boiling water. Remove and drain well.

2. In a large saucepan, cook the turnip, bacon, cream, salt, pepper and a pinch of nutmeg over a gentle heat until the turnip has absorbed quite a lot of the cream.

3. Serve piping hot on small individual plates.

TIME   Preparation takes about 8 minutes and cooking takes approximately 30 minutes.

PREPARATION   This dish can be cooked in advance and stored in the refrigerator. Reheat slowly over a gentle heat.

SERVING IDEAS   Sprinkle with chopped chives to decorate.

WATCHPOINT   Take care not to add too much salt as the bacon already gives quite a salty flavor.

☐

OPPOSITE

TURNIPS IN CREAM

SERVES 6

SMOKED HERRING SALAD

*A nouvelle cuisine recipe especially developed
for the sophisticated dinner party.*

Step 1

Step 1

☐ 4 smoked herring, filleted   ☐ 4 large new potatoes, cooked
☐ 1 onion, finely chopped   ☐ 3 Belgian endives, wiped
☐ 8 coriander seeds   ☐ ½ cup olive or corn oil
☐ 1 tsp mustard   ☐ 1 tbsp wine vinegar   ☐ 1 tsp sea salt
☐ Pepper

1. Separate the endive leaves and slice them lengthwise into thin strips.

2. Slice the herring fillets lengthwise and mix with the endive leaves.

3. Dice the potatoes, mix with the above and add the onion, coriander seeds and salt.

4. In a salad bowl, mix together the oil, mustard, vinegar and pepper.

5. Add all the other ingredients and mix well to incorporate the sauce.

TIME   Preparation takes approximately 35 minutes.

COOK'S TIP   Always store endives in semi-darkness, otherwise the leaves tend to turn green.

WATCHPOINT   Do not leave endives to soak when cleaning them, as they have a tendency to become bitter.

VARIATION   Use smoked salmon instead of smoked herring.

☐

OPPOSITE

SMOKED
HERRING SALAD

SERVES 6

FENNEL RAMEKINS

*These light fennel molds are easy to prepare and cook
and, with their aniseed flavor, provide an original dish.*

Step 1

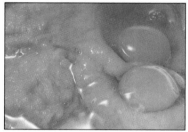

Step 3

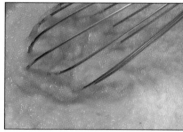

Step 3

☐ 2lbs fennel bulb, cut into quarters   ☐ 4 eggs, beaten
☐ 4 cups milk   ☐ 1 tbsp Pernod, or other aniseed alcohol
☐ ¾ cup heavy cream   ☐ Salt and pepper
☐ A little butter for greasing

1. Cut off any hard patches from the fennel and discard them. Cook the fennel in the milk for about 30 minutes, then leave to drain well.

2. Once the fennel is well drained, put the quarters into a blender and blend until smooth – this should give about 2 cups of pulp. If necessary, make up to the desired amount by adding some of the cooking milk.

3. Whisk in the eggs, aniseed, cream, salt and pepper.

4. Butter 6 ramekin dishes and fill ¾ full with the fennel mixture.

5. Place the ramekins in a high-sided dish, add water to come halfway up the sides of the ramekins, and cook in a warm oven for 30-40 minutes.

6. To serve, turn the flans out of the ramekins onto a preheated serving plate.

TIME   Preparation takes about 10 minutes, and cooking takes approximately 1 hour.

WATCHPOINT   Make sure the fennel is well cooked and that you have exactly 2 cups of the purée.

SERVING IDEAS   Serve the molds to accompany roast beef.

©Copyright F. Lebain

☐

OPPOSITE

FENNEL RAMEKINS

—————— SERVES 6 ——————

SPRING SALAD

*The very pretty "rose" in the center of this light salad
makes it a winning appetizer for a dinner party.*

Step 1

Step 2

Step 2

☐ 1 head of lettuce, washed and shredded
☐ 1 cucumber, wiped and evenly sliced
☐ 1 horseradish root, washed and evenly sliced
☐ 3 tomatoes, seeded and evenly sliced
☐ 1½ cups tuna fish, drained   ☐ 6 green onions
☐ 12 black olives, stoned   ☐ A few sprigs of fresh mint
☐ ¾ cup olive oil   ☐ 6 tbsps wine vinegar
☐ 3 drops Tabasco   ☐ Salt and pepper

1. Prepare all the vegetables, taking special care with the cucumber and horseradish as this will be the centerpiece of your finished salad.

2. On a large, round serving plate, arrange the tuna fish in a round and then form a rose shape on top of the fish by interlacing cucumber and horseradish slices.

3. In a blender or food processor, blend the olives, green onions, mint leaves, olive oil, Tabasco, vinegar, salt and pepper until smooth.

4. Place the shredded lettuce around the rose, followed by the tomatoes, and then pour over the olive/mint mixture.

TIME   Preparation takes about 45 minutes.

COOK'S TIP   Add a little more olive oil if the sauce is too thick.

SERVING IDEAS   The idea of the 'rose' presentation is optional, but the final effect is well worth the effort.

☐

OPPOSITE

SPRING SALAD

SURPRISE POTATOES

*These potatoes are an excellent and filling
accompaniment to fish dishes.*

☐ 4 ½ lbs new potatoes, steamed (but not peeled)
☐ ½ cup butter   ☐ ¾ cup heavy cream
☐ 1 red pepper, seeded and cut into thin strips
☐ 1 tbsp olive oil   ☐ Salt and pepper

Step 2

1. Cook the pepper strips in the olive oil over a high heat for a few minutes. Remove from heat and set aside.

2. Cut the potatoes in half and remove the pulp, retaining the skins.

3. Work the butter, cream, salt and pepper into the potato pulp. Stir in the pepper strips.

4. Spoon the mixture back into the skins and warm in a hot oven for 5-8 minutes. Serve piping hot.

TIME   Preparation takes about 15 minutes and cooking takes about 30 minutes, including the cooking of the potatoes.

COOK'S TIP   The potatoes can be cooked in advance and stored in the refrigerator.

VARIATION   A little grated cheese can be srpinkled over the potatoes before the final 5-8 minutes in the oven.

Step 4

☐

OPPOSITE

SURPRISE
POTATOES

SERVES 6

PETITS POIS A LA FRANÇAISE

Fresh peas cooked with onions and carrots
make a colorful vegetable combination to
accompany a wide variety of dishes.

☐ 2 ¼ lbs fresh peas (about 7lbs in the pod)
☐ 6 onions, finely chopped   ☐ 1 lettuce, finely shredded
☐ 2 carrots, peeled and finely diced   ☐ 2 tsps sugar
☐ ¼ cup butter   ☐ 1 bouquet garni   ☐ Salt and pepper

1. Rinse the peas under cold water and leave to drain.

2. In a heavy-based saucepan, melt the butter and gently cook the peas, lettuce, onion, sugar, bouquet garni, salt and pepper for 5 minutes.

3. Increase the heat, add 1 inch water, bring to the boil and add the carrots.

4. Cover the saucepan, reduce the heat to very low and cook for 15-20 minutes, or until the peas are cooked through.

5. Remove the bouquet garni and serve.

TIME   Preparation takes about 25 minutes and cooking takes approximately 20 minutes.

VARIATION   Use whole new baby carrots when they are in season.

WATCHPOINT   Check the level of water during cooking and add more if the level has dropped.

SERVING TIP   Drain the peas, if preferred, before serving and add 1 tbsp of the cooking liquid to prevent them from being too dry.

☐

OPPOSITE

PETITS POIS A LA
FRANÇAISE

—— SERVES 6 ——

GLAZED VEGETABLES

*A springtime dish that is easy to prepare and cook,
and especially good served with broiled meats.*

Step 1

Step 1

☐ 1lb carrots   ☐ 1 large cucumber   ☐ 1lb turnips
☐ 4 tbsps butter   ☐ 9 sugar cubes   ☐ Salt and pepper

1. Wash and peel the vegetables as necessary. Cut them into long olive shapes with a sharp knife.

2. Melt the butter in a large frying pan and add the vegetables, salt, pepper and sugar. Stir, adding just enough water to cover the vegetables.

3. Cook over a high heat, allowing the water to evaporate.

4. Leave the vegetables to caramelize a little and then serve. Care should be taken as some vegetables cook more quickly than others. If time permits, cook the vegetables separately.

TIME   Preparation takes about 15 minutes and cooking takes approximately 30-45 minutes.

SERVING IDEAS   Cut the vegetables into different shapes, such as thin sticks or round slices.

WATCHPOINT   Should the vegetables cook before the water has completely evaporated, remove them, place the water over a high heat to reduce and then put the vegetables back to caramelize.

☐

OPPOSITE

GLAZED
VEGETABLES

SERVES 6

SPINACH FLANS

*Delicious individual spinach flans which
are rich and light at the same time.*

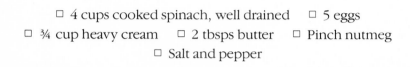

□ 4 cups cooked spinach, well drained   □ 5 eggs
□ ¾ cup heavy cream   □ 2 tbsps butter   □ Pinch nutmeg
□ Salt and pepper

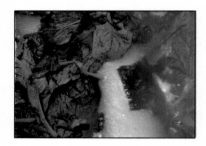

1. Preheat the oven to 300°F.

2. Squeeze out any excess water from the spinach with your fingers.

3. Add the eggs one by one to the chopped spinach, mixing well.

4. Add the cream, salt, pepper and nutmeg and mix well.

5. Grease 6 ramekin dishes with the butter, and spoon in the mixture.

6. Place the ramekins in a high-sided baking pan, pour in water to halfway up the sides and cook for approximately 40-50 minutes. Serve the flans hot.

TIME   Preparation takes about 20 minutes and cooking takes approximately 40 minutes.

VARIATION   Replace the spinach with sorrel or chard leaves.

WATCHPOINT   It is important to cook the flans in a bain marie, so that they cook gently without boiling.

□

OPPOSITE

SPINACH FLANS

—— SERVES 6 ——

CARROT PUREE

The carrot, homely classic of French cuisine, is brought to life in this recipe by the addition of cinnamon.

Step 1

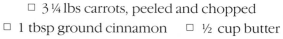

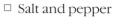

- □ 3 ¼ lbs carrots, peeled and chopped
- □ 1 tbsp ground cinnamon   □ ½ cup butter
- □ 1½ cup heavy cream   □ Juice of ½ lemon
- □ Salt and pepper

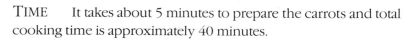

1. Cook the carrots in salted boiling water. Drain well. Push the carrots through a fine sieve or blend to a smooth purée.

2. Put the purée back on the heat in a clean saucepan.

3. Stir in the cinnamon, butter, cream, salt and pepper. Beat well with a wooden spoon and heat through.

4. Serve on a preheated dish with the lemon juice squeezed over.

TIME   It takes about 5 minutes to prepare the carrots and total cooking time is approximately 40 minutes.

WATCHPOINT   Once the cream and butter have been added, use a very gentle heat to warm the dish through.

VARIATION   The cinnamon may be omitted if it is not to your taste, but do try it as it gives a very pleasant and novel flavor.

□

OPPOSITE

CARROT PUREE

—— SERVES 6 ——

HARICOTS VERTS A LA PROVENÇALE

Fresh green beans served in the Provençale manner
make a delicious vegetable accompaniment.

Step 2

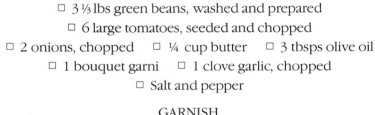

☐ 3 ⅓ lbs green beans, washed and prepared
☐ 6 large tomatoes, seeded and chopped
☐ 2 onions, chopped   ☐ ¼ cup butter   ☐ 3 tbsps olive oil
☐ 1 bouquet garni   ☐ 1 clove garlic, chopped
☐ Salt and pepper

GARNISH

☐ ½ clove garlic, chopped   ☐ 1 tbsp chopped parsley

1. In a large frying pan, heat the butter and the oil. Add the bouquet garni, garlic, tomatoes and onions and cook until very soft (20-30 minutes).

2. Cook the beans in salted boiling water until just underdone and crisp. Run them immediately under cold water to stop further cooking. Drain well and add salt and pepper.

3. Remove the bouquet garni from the tomatoes.

4. Serve the beans on a bed of the tomato purée, and sprinkle over the garlic and the parsley.

TIME   Preparation takes about 25 minutes and cooking takes approximately 35 minutes.

SERVING IDEAS   If time permits, make small baskets of the beans by gathering together 6-8 beans, with one bean tied around the middle.

COOK'S TIP   If using thick runner beans, cut them in half prior to cooking.

WATCHPOINT   Do not allow the beans to overcook. Plunge into cold water as soon as they are just done to stop the cooking process.

☐

OPPOSITE

HARICOTS VERTS A
LA PROVENÇALE

——— SERVES 6 ———

RATATOUILLE

*A rich mixture of vegetables,
equally good served hot or cold.*

Step 1

☐ 3 eggplant, washed and diced ☐ 4 zucchini, washed and diced
☐ 4 large tomatoes, wiped, seeded and diced
☐ 1 red pepper, wiped, seeded and diced
☐ 1 green pepper, wiped, seeded and diced
☐ 12 baby onions, peeled ☐ 3 cloves garlic, peeled and chopped
☐ 4 cups olive oil ☐ Sprig thyme ☐ 1 bay leaf
☐ Salt and pepper

1. Prepare all the vegetables, taking care to retain all the juice from the tomatoes when removing the seeds. Set the oil to heat in a large frying pan.

2. Fry the eggplant in the oil until just brown. Remove and drain well. Leave to drain on paper towels.

3. Fry the zucchini as above and drain well.

4. Fry the red and green peppers as above and drain well.

5. Fry the baby onions whole as above and drain well.

6. In a heavy-based saucepan, place all the cooked vegetables with the garlic, tomatoes, any tomato juice recovered during seeding, sprig of thyme, bay leaf, salt and pepper, 2 tbsps water and 2 tbsps of the frying oil. Cover and cook for 45 minutes to 1 hour over a very low heat. Stir from time to time to prevent sticking.

7. Remove the thyme and bay leaf before serving.

TIME   It will take up to 30 minutes to prepare all the vegetables. Cooking takes up to 2 hours.

WATCHPOINT   It is important to pre-fry the vegetables, as this ensures that they keep their individual flavors.

COOK'S TIP   This dish can be cooked in advance and stored in the refrigerator.

FREEZING   This dish will freeze well, but the vegetables have a tendency to become a little mushy on reheating.

☐

OPPOSITE

RATATOUILLE

PETITS POIS BONNE FEMME

*Literally 'housewife's peas', these are fresh peas enlivened
by the addition of baby onions and crispy bacon.*

□ 2 ¼ lbs fresh peas (about 7lbs in the pod)   □ 12 baby onions
□ ¼ cup butter   □ 2 tsps sugar
□ 14oz smoked bacon, chopped   □ Salt and pepper

1. Cook the chopped bacon in half of the butter, then add the peas and just enough water to cover. Cook until just done. Drain well.

2. Glaze the baby onions. To do this, cover them with water in a clean saucepan, add the sugar and the remaining butter, and season with salt and pepper. Cook over a moderate heat and stop the cooking process as soon as the juice has reduced and is lightly coating the onions (like a syrup).

3. Add the baby onions to the peas just before serving.

TIME   Preparation takes about 5 minutes and cooking takes about 30 minutes, depending on the freshness of the peas.

COOK'S TIP   This dish can be prepared in advance and stored in the refrigerator. Heat through gently before serving.

ECONOMY   Frozen peas can be used if fresh peas are not available. Cooking time will be almost identical.

□

OPPOSITE

PETITS POIS
BONNE FEMME

--- SERVES 4 ---

CRISPY GRILLED MACKEREL

*Delicious in its simplicity, this
is a particularly easy dish to prepare.*

Step 3

☐ 8 medium size fresh mackerel, gutted, washed and wiped dry
☐ 1 cup all-purpose flour   ☐ ½ cup oil   ☐ Salt

TO SERVE

☐ 2 lemons, washed, wiped and quartered
☐ 2 tbsps fresh parsley, chopped

1. Make sure the mackerel are dry: use paper towels to soak up every last drop of water.

2. Preheat the griddle or a frying pan until very hot.

3. Roll each of the fish in the flour, shaking off the excess.

4. Dip the floured fish quickly into the oil, sprinkle over the salt and then place them on the griddle or frying pan and cook until crisp – this takes approximately 15 to 20 minutes if the mackerel are of average thickness.

6. Salt lightly before serving.

TIME   Preparation takes about 20 minutes and cooking takes approximately 20 minutes.

SERVING IDEA   Serve with Maitre d'Hotel butter.

WATCHPOINT   Make sure that the griddle or frying pan is very hot.

☐

OPPOSITE

CRISPY GRILLED
MACKEREL

SCALLOPS WITH FRESH BASIL

An easy recipe that is quick to prepare and cook; perhaps a little expensive, but an absolutely delicious treat.

Step 1

Step 2

Step 2

- ☐ 18 scallops, rinsed, dried and halved
- ☐ 10 fresh basil leaves, wiped and finely chopped
- ☐ 8 Belgian endives ☐ 2 cloves garlic, finely chopped
- ☐ ½ cup butter ☐ Salt and pepper

1. Separate the endive leaves and cut them lengthwise into thin strips. Cook them in a frying pan in half of the butter and a little salt and pepper until quite tender.

2. In a clean frying pan, melt the remaining butter, add the garlic and basil, and cook for a few minutes. Turn the heat up to high and sauté the scallops in the mixture, first on one side and then on the other. Add a little salt and pepper.

3. Serve the scallops in their sauce over a bed of warm endives.

TIME   It takes about 5 to 8 minutes to prepare the endives and cooking takes approximately 25 minutes in total.

TIME SAVER   The endives can be cooked in advance, stored in the refrigerator and reheated gently before serving.

WATCHPOINT   Do not cook the scallops in advance as they tend to harden when reheated.

☐

OPPOSITE

SCALLOPS WITH
FRESH BASIL

──── SERVES 6 ────

SEA BREAM WITH PEPPERCORN SAUCE

A light, peppery sauce, delicately flavored with aniseed, brings new life to the rather bland flavor of sea bream.

□ 2 large gray sea bream, skinned, gutted, filleted, rinsed and wiped dry □ 10 green peppercorns
□ 10 pink peppercorns (baies roses)
□ 1 tomato, seeded and chopped □ 2 shallots, chopped
□ ½ cup white wine
□ 1 jigger of Noilly Pratt or other aniseed alcohol
□ 1 tbsp cognac □ 1 tbsp sugar □ 1 tbsp olive oil
□ 1 cup heavy cream

1. Heat the olive oil in a frying pan and sauté the peppercorns. Pour off the oil, deglaze the frying pan with the cognac, and add the shallots, tomato, aniseed alcohol, white wine and the sugar. Stir well and allow the mixture to thicken until quite syrupy. This may take quite a while if the tomato was very juicy.

2. Whilst the sauce is thickening, cook the fish fillets under a hot broiler. An oven broiler is best for this.

3. Stir the cream into the sauce over a very gentle heat, ensuring that the sauce does not boil.

4. Using a hand mixer, blend the sauce until smooth and serve poured over the hot fish.

TIME   Preparation takes 20 minutes and cooking takes a further 35 to 40 minutes.

VARIATION   Any firm-fleshed fish could be used for this recipe instead of the sea bream.

COOK'S TIP   Note that this recipe does not call for any salt as the aniseed liquor gives a particular flavor. If you wish, allow guests to season their own serving once they have tasted the sauce.

SERVING IDEA   Serve the fish with ratatouille, as each dish complements the other.

VARIATION   Substitute dry vermouth for the Noilly Pratt.

□

OPPOSITE

SEA BREAM WITH
PEPPERCORN
SAUCE

SERVES 4

MOULES MARINIERE

Mussels cooked in white wine: one of the best-known traditional French dishes.

Step 1

Step 1

Step 1

□ 12 cups mussels, pre-soaked for 1 hour in salted water
□ 1 large onion, thinly sliced   □ 2 cloves garlic, chopped
□ 2 sprigs parsley, rinsed   □ 4 cups white wine
□ ¼ cup butter   □ Salt and pepper

TO SERVE

□ 3 tbsps fresh parsley, chopped

1. Drain the mussels. Scrape off any persistent sand and rinse the mussels thoroughly in cold running water. Remove any stringy parts.

2. In a large saucepan, cook the mussels, onion, garlic, sprigs of parsley, half of the butter, salt and pepper for 4 minutes. Pour over the wine and cook for a further 8 minutes.

3. Take the saucepan off of the heat and remove the mussels with a slotted spoon. Allow them to cool a little and remove the mussels from the opened shells. Discard any that have not opened. Keep a few shells for decoration and discard the rest.

4. Keep the mussels warm.

5. Remove the sprigs of parsley from the cooking liquid and drain it through a fine cheesecloth. Return the drained liquid to the saucepan over a high heat and bring to the boil. Allow to reduce by at least a third.

6. Stir in the remaining butter and a little more salt and pepper to taste. Stir in the mussels and the reserved shells. Serve hot.

TIME   The mussels need to be soaked for an hour. Preparation takes 5 minutes and cooking takes appoximately 35 minutes.

COOK'S TIP   Buy the smallest mussels you can find as they tend to have a richer flavor than the large variety.

TIME SAVER   The dish can be cooked in advance up to Step 6, and then reheated before serving, adding the remaining butter.

VARIATION   Stir 2 tbsps heavy cream into the sauce before serving.

□

OPPOSITE

MOULES
MARINIERE

———— SERVES 6 ————

BRANDADE DE MORUE

*This very rich and filling fish paste
needs to be begun a day in advance.*

Step 2

☐ 2 ¼ lbs salt cod ☐ 2 cups olive oil ☐ 1 cup heavy cream
☐ Pepper

1. Soak the salt cod for one day in cold water, changing the water frequently to remove the excess salt.

2. Poach the fish for 7 minutes on a high heat. Drain well. Remove all the bones and the skin, and flake the flesh very finely.

3. In a large saucepan, gently heat about ⅕ of the oil and add the fish, stirring well until a fine paste is reached.

4. Remove from the heat and, using a spatula, briskly work in the remaining oil and the cream, adding them alternately, drop by drop. Season well with pepper.

TIME   Preparation takes about 15 minutes, cooking takes 40 minutes and the soaking of the salt cod takes at least one day.

SERVING IDEA   Serve the brandade with small croutons rubbed with a clove of garlic and a little tomato sauce.

WATCHPOINT   When incorporating the oil and the cream it is important to work the mixture vigorously.

☐

OPPOSITE

BRANDADE
DE MORUE

---- SERVES 6 ----

GRILLED TUNA STEAKS

*Delicious grilled tuna steaks make for great
barbeque food and are so much more sophisticated
than sausages or chops.*

Step 1

Step 1

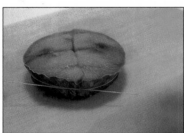

Step 1

☐ 6 slices of fresh tuna   ☐ 2 tbsps herbes de Provence
☐ 4 tbsps olive oil

TO SERVE

☐ 1 tomato   ☐ 1 tbsp fresh herbs, chopped   ☐ 2 tbsp olive oil
☐ 1 tbsp vinegar   ☐ Salt and pepper

1. Remove the bones from the tuna slices, roll the fish into rounds and secure with kitchen string. Cut out the central bone and the side bones from the slices of fish. Secure into rounds with kitchen string.

2. Place on a shallow plate and pour over the olive oil.

3. Sprinkle over the herbes de Provence and place in the refrigerator for at least 3 hours.

4. Preheat the griddle, frying pan or barbeque until very hot and cook the fish until crispy on the outside and just slightly red in the center.

5. Peel the tomato and chop into small cubes.

6. Make a vinaigrette sauce by mixing together the vinegar, oil and the herbs. Season well with salt and pepper. Stir in the tomato and serve at the side of the fish.

TIME   Preparation takes about 15 minutes and marinating takes at least 3 hours. Cooking takes about 15 minutes.

SERVING IDEA   Make up another measure of the tomato vinaigrette sauce and serve it over a mixed salad.

WATCHPOINT   Should the steaks be very thick and you are using a griddle or frying pan, just color the fish under a high heat and then finish cooking in the oven to avoid burning.

☐

OPPOSITE

GRILLED TUNA
STEAKS

—— SERVES 4 ——

SKATE WITH CAPER SAUCE

*Experiment with the capers in this sauce to achieve
the flavor that is to your liking.*

☐ 2 ¼ lbs skate, skinned and filleted
☐ 20 capers in vinegar, drained   ☐ 2 lemons, peeled and diced
☐ 5 slices white bread, toasted and diced into croûtons
☐ 1 onion, chopped   ☐ 1 carrot, chopped   ☐ 1 leek, chopped
☐ 1 tbsp thyme   ☐ 2 bay leaves   ☐ 1 cup fish stock
☐ ⅔ cup heavy cream   ☐ Salt and pepper

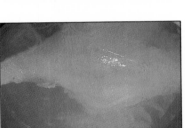

Step 2

1. Bring to the boil 1 cup water with the onion, carrot, leek, salt, pepper, thyme and bay leaves. Simmer gently for 10 minutes.

2. Once this vegetable stock is ready, add the skate and simmer gently for approximately 8 minutes – less if the fillets are very thin.

3. Heat the fish stock in a separate saucepan with the capers for about 3 minutes. Remove from the heat, allow to cool a little and then blend in a blender or food processor until smooth. Beat in the cream. Return to a high heat and allow to reduce and thicken. Stir the sauce from time to time to prevent lumps from forming. Just before serving the sauce, blend with a hand mixer to make sure that it is very smooth.

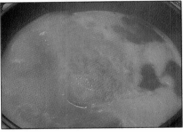

Step 2

4. Serve the skate cut into small pieces on a preheated serving dish with the sauce poured over. Sprinkle over the diced lemon and the croûtons.

TIME   Preparation takes 15 minutes and cooking takes about 25 minutes.

VARIATION   More capers can be added if liked.

COOK'S TIP   It is very important to remove all the bones from the fillets. This can be a long, delicate job, and tweezers are often a help.

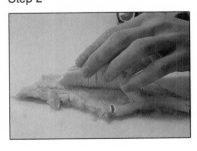

☐

OPPOSITE

SKATE WITH
CAPER SAUCE

SERVES 8

BOUILLABAISSE

A hearty fish dish for a soup or main course, ideal for dinner on a cold winter's evening. This dish originally comes from the South of France, where the aioli (garlic) sauce is served in a small bowl for guests to help themselves.

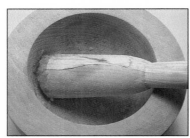
Step 3

Step 3

Step 3

Step 3

☐ 9lbs mixed fish and shell fish, such as cod, whiting, red mullet, crab, mussels   ☐ 1 sprig fennel   ☐ 2 large potatoes, diced   ☐ 3 cloves garlic   ☐ 6 tomatoes   ☐ 1 onion, finely chopped   ☐ 6 tbsps olive oil   ☐ 1 tsp thyme   ☐ 1 bay leaf   ☐ Pinch saffron   ☐ Salt and pepper

AIOLI SAUCE

☐ 4 cloves garlic   ☐ 1 hot red pepper (optional)   ☐ ½ potato, cooked   ☐ 1 egg yolk   ☐ ½ cup olive oil   ☐ Salt and pepper

1. Scale and fillet the fish and cut it into chunks, retaining the bones. Rinse the shellfish well.

2. Heat the oil in a very large saucepan. Cook the onion, garlic, fennel, fish bones, crab and mussels (if being used). Cover with water, and stir in the thyme, bay leaf and the saffron. Then add the diced potatoes. Cook for 1½ hours, checking the level of water from time to time and adding more as necessary.

3. Meanwhile, make the sauce. Crush the garlic, salt and pepper with a mortar and pestle. Add the potato and then the egg yolk. Mix well and then thicken with the olive oil, adding it drop by drop. If using hot red pepper, add it to taste at the last moment.

4. Strain the soup through a fine sieve and add plenty of salt and pepper.

5. Add the cubes of fish to the soup and cook for a further 5 minutes before serving.

TIME   Preparation takes about 15 minutes and cooking takes 1 hour and 30 minutes.

ECONOMY   Extra potato can be substituted for some of the fish to make the soup go further.

SERVING IDEA   Serve with croutons that have been rubbed with a clove of garlic.

☐

OPPOSITE

BOUILLABAISSE

---- SERVES 6 ----

BOW TIE SOLE FILLETS
IN OYSTER SAUCE

*With the rich flavor of oyster sauce, this is an imaginative
way of serving sole – an ideal dinner party dish.*

Step 1

☐ 3 sole fillets ☐ 2 cups fish stock
☐ 2 cups mushrooms, rinsed, wiped and finely sliced
☐ 12 oysters, shells removed ☐ 2 tomatoes, wiped and diced
☐ 3 tbsps heavy cream ☐ Salt and pepper

1. Cut the sole fillets lengthwise into two and tie each piece into a knot, this makes the 'bow tie'.

2. In a large frying pan, cook the mushrooms and half of the tomatoes in the stock for 5 minutes.

3. Gently lower the 'bow ties' into the stock and cook gently for about 5 more minutes – cooking time will depend on the thickness of the fillets.

4. Carefully remove the cooked fillets with the help of a slotted spoon. Remove the sauce from the heat and stir in the cream.

5. Arrange the 'bow ties' neatly on a preheated serving dish.

6. Blend the sauce with a hand mixer until smooth. Stir the oysters into the sauce just prior to serving. Allow just enough time to heat the oysters through and pour immediately over the 'bow ties'. Sprinkle over the remaining diced tomato. Serve immediately.

TIME   Preparation takes about 10 minutes and total cooking time is about 30 minutes.

COOK'S TIP   Use the very best quality oysters on the market, they make all the difference to this dish. They should be firm, with not to much juice in the shell.

WATCHPOINT   The oysters should be cooked for a maximum of 2 minutes, otherwise they will shrink.

©Copyright F. Lebain.

Step 1

☐

OPPOSITE

BOW TIE SOLE
FILLETS IN
OYSTER SAUCE

RED MULLET WITH CHIVES

With its bright red fish and green sauce,
this dish is a certain eye-catcher

□ 6 red mullet, gutted, skinned, washed, wiped and filleted
□ 6 tbsps fresh chives, chopped   □ 1 cup heavy cream
□ 1 cup fish stock   □ 1 tbsp olive oil   □ Salt and pepper

1. Prepare the fish, making sure that all the bones have been removed.

2. In a saucepan over a brisk heat, reduce the fish stock by half, stir in the cream and reduce a little further. Stir in three-quarters of the chives and blend with a hand mixer until smooth.

3. Season the sauce with a little salt and pepper.

4. Heat the olive oil in a large frying pan and fry the mullet fillets until cooked through and slightly crisp.

5. Reheat the sauce, but do not allow it to boil.

6. Serve the fillets on a bed of the sauce.

TIME   Preparation takes 5 minutes and cooking takes about 25 minutes.

SERVING IDEA   Garnish the dish with fresh chives.

Step 1

Step 4

□

OPPOSITE

RED MULLET
WITH CHIVES

ROLLED SOLE FILLETS

*An absolute delight to the eye and palate, these delicate
sole rolls, with their herb stuffing and mushroom sauce,
are sure winners every time.*

Step 1

Step 2

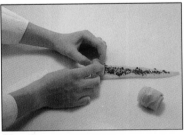

Step 2

□ 12 small sole fillets
□ 2 tbsps fresh herbs, chopped (parsley, chive, basil etc.)
□ 2 cups fish stock   □ 1 cup heavy cream
□ 2 cups mushrooms, rinsed, wiped and chopped
□ 1 clove garlic, chopped   □ Salt and pepper

1. Beat the sole fillets flat, between 2 sheets of plastic wrap, with light strokes of a rolling pin.

2. Sprinkle the fresh herbs over the fish and then roll up the fillets.

3. In a saucepan over a high heat, boil the stock and allow to reduce by half. Add the mushrooms and garlic and cook for a further 8 minutes. Remove from the heat, beat in the cream and add a little salt and pepper. Remove the mushrooms and set them aside for Step 6.

4. Remove the saucepan from the heat and allow the stock to cool a little. Blend until smooth in a blender.

5. Meanwhile, steam the fish rolls until cooked – approximately 8 minutes.

6. Replace the mushrooms and reheat the sauce, but do not let it boil.

7. Serve the sole rolls on a warmed serving dish with the sauce poured over.

TIME   It takes about 15 minutes to prepare all the ingredients. Cooking takes about 30 minutes.

COOK'S TIP   The fillets can be gently tied with fine kitchen string at the end of Step 2 – this will help them to keep their shape whilst cooking. Do not forget to remove the strings before serving.

MICROWAVE TIP   The fish can be prepared in advance and reheated in the microwave before serving.

WATCHPOINT   The sauce should be made just prior to serving. Do not allow it to boil.

□

OPPOSITE

ROLLED
SOLE FILLETS

GRILLED TROUT

A quick and easy recipe for trout, this is one of the most popular ways of serving this fish in France.

Step 1

Step 1

☐ 6 river trout, gutted, washed and wiped   ☐ 2 tbsps olive oil
☐ ⅝ cup (small pot) fresh fish roe   ☐ Juice of 1 lemon
☐ Salt and pepper

1. Begin by preparing the trout. Cut off their fins, scale them, gut them, wash well under running water and dry them on paper towels.

2. If using an oven broiler, set it to high, or heat up a flat griddle or skillet.

3. Dip the trout in the olive oil and sprinkle them with salt and pepper. Cook the fish until nicely marked on the outside and just tender on the inside.

4. Pour a little lemon juice on each fish and serve hot with a spoonful of fish roe on the top.

TIME   It will take about 10 minutes to prepare the fish and approximately 20 minutes to cook them, depending on their thickness.

SERVING IDEA   If you are serving the trout for a dinner party, use caviar instead of ordinary roe, omitting the salt in Step 3.

COOK'S TIP   If using a traditional flat griddle, heat it until very hot and mark the fish by searing first in one direction and then turning the fish 90° and searing again. You can then finish cooking in a moderate oven.

☐

OPPOSITE

GRILLED TROUT

TROUT FILLETS WITH
FISH ROE SAUCE

*The original folding of the trout fillets during the preparation
provides another visually appealing dish.*

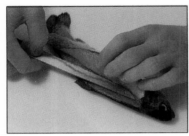

Step 1

Step 1

Step 1

☐ 4 trout, filleted   ☐ 4 tbsps fish roe   ☐ 1 cup fish stock
☐ ½ cup light cream   ☐ Salt and pepper

1. Remove the fillets from the trout, cut them in two and then place them on a sheet of plastic wrap, one piece skin side up, the next flesh side up. Sprinkle with salt and pepper and then close the packet of plastic wrap around the fish.

2. Put the stock in a saucepan over a high heat and allow to reduce by half. Stir in the cream and allow to reduce a little more. Process in a blender and keep warm over a saucepan of hot water.

3. Steam the fish in their packets until cooked, then remove the plastic wrap.

4. Serve on a hot plate with the sauce poured around the fish and the roe sprinkled over.

TIME   Preparation takes about 10 minutes, and cooking takes 40 minutes.

WATCHPOINT   Do not add a lot of salt to the sauce or to the fish as the fish roe is already quite salty.

VARIATION   For the special occasion, replace the fish roe with caviar.

☐

OPPOSITE

TROUT FILLETS
WITH FISH ROE
SAUCE

—— SERVES 4 ——

TROUT FILLETS WITH HERBS

Marinated fillets of trout cooked with a crispy herb shell,
with an accompaniment of buttered spinach.

Step 3

Step 3

Step 4

□ 4 trout, cut into fillets   □ 2 tbsps fresh herbs, chopped
□ 6 tbsps olive oil   □ Juice of 1 lemon
□ 5 tbsps fresh breadcrumbs   □ 1 clove garlic, finely chopped
□ ¾ cup fish stock   □ 6 tbsps light cream
□ 2 cups spinach leaves, washed, dried and chopped
□ 1 tbsp butter   □ 1 tbsp oil melted with 1 nut butter
□ 2 tbsps chopped tomato

1. Mix the oil with the lemon juice and marinate the fillets in the mixture for 1 hour.

2. Mix together the garlic, herbs and the breadcrumbs.

3. Drain the fillets and toss in the herbed breadcrumbs.

4. Heat the oil and butter in a frying pan, place in the fillets and cook them gently, skin side first, then turn the fillets over, raise the heat and crisp up the other side. Allow to reach a nice golden-brown color.

5. Meanwhile, sauté the spinach leaves in the butter, taking care not to overcook – they should still be crispy.

6. Place the stock in a saucepan, allow to reduce by half, remove from the heat and stir in the cream.

7. Blend the sauce in a blender until smooth.

8. Serve the spinach next to the crisp fillets, with the sauce poured around the spinach and the tomato dotted over.

TIME   Preparation takes about 30 minutes, marinating time is 1 hour and cooking takes approximately 40 minutes.

VARIATION   This recipe can be prepared using other fish, for example salmon.

SERVING IDEA   New baby carrots, cooked until slightly crisp, are delicious with this recipe.

□

OPPOSITE

TROUT FILLETS
WITH HERBS

— SERVES 6 —

MACKEREL WITH PEPPERCORNS

Smoked fish is very popular in France. This recipe is so quick to prepare that it has become a housewife's favorite.

Step 2

☐ 3 whole smoked mackerel with peppercorns, halved
☐ 1 tbsp wine vinegar ☐ 3 tbsps olive oil
☐ 3 shallots, finely chopped
☐ 2 tomatoes, skinned, seeded and diced
☐ 2 sprigs of fresh fennel, snipped
☐ 1 fancy-leaved lettuce, washed and dried ☐ Salt and pepper

1. Make the vinaigrette sauce by beating together the vinegar, salt, pepper, oil and the shallots.

2. Cut the mackerel into fairly thick slices.

3. Place the prepared lettuce on a serving plate, add the slices of mackerel and pour over the vinaigrette sauce.

4. Decorate the plate with the diced tomato and the snipped fennel sprigs.

TIME   Preparation takes about 15 minutes.

VARIATION   The mackerel can be replaced with any other smoked fish.

VARIATION   Experiment with the choice of salad; try using the red-leaved varieties now readily available.

☐

OPPOSITE

MACKEREL WITH PEPPERCORNS

—— SERVES 6 ——

HARLEQUIN SCALLOPS

*The scallop is of the same family as the coquille
St. Jacques. This particularly attractive dish
is perfect for the special occasion.*

Step 1

Step 1

□ 54 scallops
□ 1 red pepper, wiped, seeded and cut into small cubes
□ 1 green pepper, wiped, seeded and cut into small cubes
□ 1 stick celery, cut into small cubes
□ 2 carrots, peeled and cut into small cubes
□ 2 tbsps olive oil   □ 1 clove garlic, finely chopped
□ 1 pinch thyme   □ Salt and pepper

1. Open the scallops, remove the part which holds the scallop to the shell and then slide all the scallops onto a plate. Keep cool.

2. Warm the oil in a large frying pan with the garlic, and add all the vegetables and the scallops. Add a little salt and pepper and the thyme. Cook very gently for 10 minutes, stirring frequently.

3. After cooking, the vegetables should still be quite crisp. Fill each shell with a little of the mixture and then put them in a hot oven to heat through completely.

4. Serve piping hot.

TIME   Preparation takes about 30 minutes and cooking will also take about 30 minutes.

WATCHPOINT   Take care in preparing the vegetables, they should be cut into very small cubes (brunaise). This way they remain quite crisp during cooking. Vegetables and scallops should be cooked over a very gentle heat.

©Copyright F. Lebain.

□

OPPOSITE

HARLEQUIN
SCALLOPS

SERVES 6

CRAB SALAD WITH RUM

A lovely light salad to make when fresh crab is available.
The dish can also be made with canned crab meat.

Step 3

Step 3

☐ 1 large can crab meat, drained ☐ 2 avocados
☐ 4 artichoke hearts
☐ 1 head lettuce, washed, dried and shredded
☐ 3 sticks celery, wiped, strings removed and diced
☐ Juice of 2 lemons

SAUCE

☐ 1 egg yolk ☐ ½ cup oil ☐ 2 tsps mustard
☐ 4 tbsps light cream ☐ 1 tbsp chopped parsley
☐ A jigger of rum ☐ Salt and pepper

---

1. Have the lemon juice ready. Peel the avocado pears and, with a melon baller, scoop out the flesh. Dip the balls immediately into the lemon juice, then place them in a bowl in the refrigerator.

2. Dice the artichoke hearts and dip them into the lemon juice. Put them in the refrigerator with the avocado balls.

3. Make the sauce by beating the egg yolk with the mustard. Beat in the oil, drop by drop, then beat in the cream, rum, parsley, salt and pepper.

4. Place a small bed of lettuce on 6 individual plates, and top with the avocado, artichoke and the diced celery. Break up the crab meat and scatter over the salad.

5. Serve with the rum sauce dotted over.

TIME   Preparation takes about 30 minutes.

SERVING IDEA   If time and budget permit, use fresh crab cooked in fish stock.

WATCHPOINT   Do not cut the avocado or the artichoke too far in advance of serving, as even with the lemon juice they tend to discolor.

☐

OPPOSITE

CRAB SALAD
WITH RUM

MARINATED HERRINGS

*A dish to prepare in advance and serve on warm
summer evenings, or perhaps on picnics.*

Step 1

Step 1

□ 4 cups olive oil   □ 6 smoked herrings, cut into small fillets
□ 2 onions, sliced   □ 6 bay leaves
□ 1 carrot, scraped and thinly sliced   □ 10 coriander seeds

1. Put half the onion, coriander, bay leaves and carrot in a terrine. Interleave the herring fillets among them. Cover with the remaining half of the vegetables and herbs and pour the olive oil over.

2. Leave to marinate in a cool place for at least 2 days.

3. Serve either directly from the terrine, or cut into smaller pieces on individual plates. Add a slice of tomato and a few leaves of salad and spoon over a little of the marinade.

TIME   Preparation takes about 20 minutes, plus at least 2 days marinating time.

VARIATION   The addition of fresh herbs, such as parsley or chives, adds not only color but a distinctive flavor as well.

SERVING IDEAS   Serve with crisp French stick with lots of butter.

COOK'S TIP   This dish can be made up to 2 weeks in advance and kept in the fridge.

□

OPPOSITE

MARINATED
HERRINGS

―――― SERVES 4 ――――

COD WITH LEEKS

Large slices of cod are required for this dish. Keep the skin on the fish for an attractive presentation.

Step 1

Step 2

Step 3

□ 2lbs leeks, well rinsed and drained □ 2 thick pieces of cod
□ 1½ cups light cream □ Salt and pepper
□ 1 tbsp fresh chives, chopped

1. Cut each piece of cod into two, removing any bones. Sprinkle with salt and pepper and keep in a cool place.

2. Cut the leeks into very fine slices, put them in a frying pan and pour over the cream. Cook on a very gentle heat for 10 minutes, covered.

3. Add the fish to the leeks and continue cooking for 10 minutes.

4. Serve the leek and cream base on a pre-heated plate with the fillets placed on top and the chives sprinkled over.

TIME   Preparation takes about 5 minutes, and cooking takes 20 minutes.

WATCHPOINT   Check during cooking that the cream has not evaporated too quickly. If this should be the case add a little more cream.

VARIATION   This dish can be prepared with other types of fish if cod is not available

©Copyright F. Lebain.

□

<u>OPPOSITE</u>

COD WITH LEEKS

---— SERVES 6 ——---

CALAMARS DE PROVENCE

A traditional recipe for squid from the South of France.

Step 1

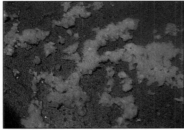

Step 2

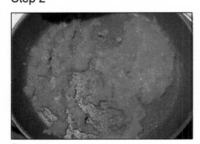

Step 2

Step 3

- ☐ 5 ½ lbs squid, washed and cut into thin slices
- ☐ 5 onions, chopped   ☐ 5 cloves garlic, chopped
- ☐ 5 tomatoes, chopped   ☐ 1 cup white wine   ☐ 1 cup fish stock
- ☐ 1 tbsp heavy cream   ☐ 1 pinch saffron   ☐ 1 tbsp olive oil
- ☐ 1 tsp cayenne pepper   ☐ 1 bouquet garni
- ☐ 1 tsp fennel seeds (optional)   ☐ Salt and pepper

1. Warm the oil in a frying pan and cook the squid and fennel seeds until all the juices evaporate.

2. Remove the squid and add the onion, garlic, cayenne pepper, bouquet garni and the tomatoes. Stir well and cook for a few minutes.

3. Pour over the stock and the wine, sprinkle over the saffron, and stir well. Cook on a fairly brisk heat until the sauce has reduced somewhat. Return the squid to the pan.

4. Reduce the heat, cover and cook very gently until the squid is tender.

5. Just before serving, remove the bouquet garni and stir in the cream. Check the seasoning and add a little salt and pepper if necessary.

TIME   Preparation takes about 25 minutes and cooking takes approximately 40 minutes.

WATCHPOINT   Should the cream separate when you add it to the sauce, pour the sauce into a blender, add some light cream and blend until smooth.

SERVING IDEA   Serve with whole brown rice or Rice Pilaf.

☐

OPPOSITE

CALAMARS
DE PROVENCE

——— SERVES 4 ———

STUFFED SQUID

*The light, tasty stuffing for this dish really enhances the flavor
of the squid. Squid is a very popular dish in the South of France.*

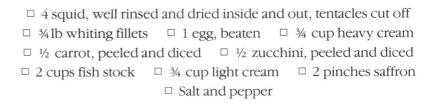

☐ 4 squid, well rinsed and dried inside and out, tentacles cut off
☐ ¾ lb whiting fillets ☐ 1 egg, beaten ☐ ¾ cup heavy cream
☐ ½ carrot, peeled and diced ☐ ½ zucchini, peeled and diced
☐ 2 cups fish stock ☐ ¾ cup light cream ☐ 2 pinches saffron
☐ Salt and pepper

Step 3

1. To make the stuffing, first grind the whiting fillets with 1 tbsp light cream and the beaten egg in a mixer or food processor. Add salt and pepper.

2. Blanch the carrot and zucchini cubes in boiling water for 2 minutes and add to the ground whiting. Stir well to mix evenly.

3. Whip the heavy cream and gently fold into the fish stuffing.

Step 4

4. Stuff the squid with the whiting mixture, forcing it well down. Sew the ends up with fine kitchen thread and steam-cook the squid for 15 minutes.

5. Heat the stock in a saucepan, allowing it to reduce by three-quarters. Stir in the remaining light cream and the saffron. Allow to reduce a little more and then blend until smooth.

6. Cut the squid into slices and serve with the sauce poured over.

TIME   Preparation takes about 20 minutes and cooking takes approximately 1 hour.

SERVING IDEA   Sprinkle over 2 tbsps fresh chives, chopped.

COOK'S TIP   Use a pastry bag with a large tip to stuff the squid neatly.

ECONOMY   Use frozen squid instead of fresh and you can cook this dish all year round.

Step 4

☐

OPPOSITE

STUFFED SQUID

SERVES 6

BRAISED DUCKLING WITH TURNIP SAUCE

An original idea for using turnips – the duckling is complemented marvelously by the turnip flavoring.

Step 1

Step 2

□ 1 large duckling   □ 3 ⅓ lbs turnips, peeled and sliced
□ 3 onions, sliced   □ Juice of 3 large turnips   □ 1 clove garlic
□ 1 bouquet garni   □ Salt and pepper

1. Cut the duckling into pieces and brown in a casserole without adding any more fat. Add the sliced turnips and continue cooking.

2. Once the duckling has become slightly transparent, add 2 tbsps water, the onions, turnip juice, garlic, bouquet garni, salt and pepper. Cook over a very low heat for 20 to 30 minutes.

3. Remove the bouquet garni, the duckling pieces and the turnip.

4. Putting back up to half of the turnips little by little, blend with the juices using a mixer or food processor until smooth and as thick as desired.

5. Serve on a pre-heated plate, interlacing the duckling pieces with the remaining turnip slices, and pour the sauce around the edge.

TIME   Preparation takes about 30 minutes, and cooking takes approximately 45 minutes.

VARIATION   Barbary duck or mallard will provide a stronger flavored alternative to duckling.

□

OPPOSITE

BRAISED
DUCKLING WITH
TURNIP SAUCE

DUCK IN ORANGE SAUCE

*A great French classic, duck has always been very popular
in France, and wild duck is much sought after.*

Step 1

Step 1

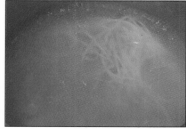

Step 6

☐

OPPOSITE

DUCK IN ORANGE
SAUCE

☐ 1 large duck, prepared, dried and cut into pieces
☐ 1 carrot, scraped and shredded ☐ 1 onion, finely chopped
☐ 8 oranges, washed and dried ☐ 5 tbsps butter
☐ 1 tbsp vinegar ☐ 1 tbsp cornstarch, dissolved in 1 tbsp water
☐ Salt and pepper

1. Peel 2 of the oranges with a potato peeler and cut the peel into fine strips. Blanch the strips in boiling water for a few minutes, drain well and set aside. Retain the oranges for the juice.

2. Peel 4 more oranges and cut the flesh into thick slices.

3. Melt ⅔ of the butter in a heavy casserole and brown the duck pieces on all sides. Reduce the heat, add the onion, carrot and 2 tbsps water. Cover and cook for about 30 minutes, turning the duck pieces from time to time. Add a little water if necessary during cooking.

4. Remove the duck pieces from the casserole and wrap up tightly in aluminum foil. Strain the juices from the casserole through a fine sieve and pour into a clean saucepan.

5. Squeeze the juice of the peeled oranges and the remaining 2 oranges, add this to the strained casserole juices and stir well. Add the vinegar and the orange strips. Cook over a low heat for a few minutes.

6. Stir in the dissolved cornstarch, stirring continuously until the sauce begins to thicken. Remove from the heat and keep warm.

7. Cut the meat off the duck and present it on a serving dish.

8. In a clean saucepan, cook the orange slices in the remaining butter until they have taken on a little color. Add the sauce, stir and serve poured over the duck pieces.

TIME   Preparation takes 50 minutes and cooking takes about 1 hour.

VARIATION   Try using blood oranges; they have more flavor and add much more color.

WATCHPOINT   When adding the cornstarch to the sauce, stir continuously to prevent lumps from forming.

TIME SAVER   The duck can be cooked in advance and frozen, although the sauce is best made on the day of serving.

SERVES 6

TURKEY WITH FRESH TARRAGON

This is quite an economical turkey recipe, and a particularly tasty one with its fresh, herby sauce.

□ 3 large turkey breasts □ 2 tbsps fresh tarragon, chopped
□ 6 tbsps heavy cream □ 1 cup chicken stock
□ 2 tbsps port □ 1 tbsp cornstarch, dissolved in 1 tbsp water
□ 2 tbsps oil □ 1 nut butter □ Salt and pepper

Step 1

Step 1

1. Sprinkle the turkey breasts with salt and pepper and then cook in a casserole dish in the oil and butter until lightly browned.

2. Pour off any excess fat, add the tarragon, port and stock, and stir well. Bring to the boil, reduce very slightly and allow to cook until the juices reduce by about a third.

3. Place the casserole dish in a moderately hot oven to finish cooking.

4. When the turkey is cooked through and ready to serve, remove the breasts and set aside. Stir in the dissolved cornstarch, stirring continuously, until the sauce thickens. Stir in the cream.

5. Cut the breasts into thin slices and serve with the sauce poured over.

TIME   Preparation takes about 5 minutes and cooking takes 30 minutes, perhaps a little longer if the breasts are very thick.

SERVING IDEA   Serve with a nice, bright vegetable purée, such as carrot or fresh peas.

□

OPPOSITE

TURKEY WITH
FRESH TARRAGON

POULE AU RIZ

*This classic chicken dish from Alsace is served on a
bed of rice with a rich, creamy sauce.*

Step 2

Step 2

Step 3

Step 3

□

OPPOSITE

POULE AU RIZ

□ 1 large stewing chicken, cleaned and dried
□ Juice of 1 lemon   □ 1 onion, chopped
□ 1 carrot, chopped   □ 1 leek, chopped
□ 1 stick celery, finely chopped   □ 1 bouquet garni
□ ¼ cup butter   □ ½ cup flour
□ 1 cup heavy cream   □ Salt and pepper
□ 6 portions of cooked long grain rice

1. Put the chicken in a large saucepan and cover with cold water. Bring to the boil and as soon as the water is boiling well, remove the bird and drain well.

2. Separate the wings, thighs and the breasts. Sprinkle the lemon juice over the pieces of meat. Break up the carcass.

3. Put the carcass bones back into the saucepan, cover with water, and add all the vegetables, the bouquet garni and the pieces of meat. Bring to the boil, cover, reduce the heat and simmer until the meat is tender.

4. Remove the pieces of meat and keep them warm. Boil what remains in the saucepan and allow it to reduce.

5. Skim off any fat that rises to the top. Strain the sauce through a fine sieve and discard everything but the strained liquid.

6. In another saucepan, melt the butter and stir in the flour. Stir in the juices and continue stirring until the sauce thickens. Cook for a few minutes more and then stir in the cream and add salt and pepper.

7. Serve the pieces of chicken on a bed of rice with the sauce poured over.

TIME   Preparation takes about 15 minutes and cooking takes 1 hour.

COOK'S TIP   Whenever cooking a stewing chicken, always bring it to the boil in the above manner before using it in a recipe. It helps to remove excess fat and makes the bird much more digestible.

WATCHPOINT   At Step 5, when you are skimming off the fat, wipe the sides of the saucepan with damp kitchen paper, so that when you pour out the juices you do not take any fat with them.

─────── SERVES 6 ───────

SLICED CHICKEN
WITH FIGS

*A new recipe that presents chicken in a new light –
this recipe will delight all who taste it.*

- 1 large chicken, boned and cut into slices
- 1 cup white wine   □ 1 cup chicken stock
- 1 small stick cinnamon   □ 15 coriander seeds
- 2 tsps honey   □ 6 dried figs, each cut into 3
- 1 tbsp oil   □ ¼ cup butter
- Pinch of saffron   □ Salt and pepper

1. In a heavy frying pan, melt the butter and the oil and fry the chicken slices. Allow to brown slightly, then take off the heat.

2. Remove the chicken from the frying pan and keep it warm. Put the frying pan back on the heat and add the cinnamon, wine, stock, saffron, coriander, figs, honey, salt and pepper. Stir well and cook for 4 minutes. Return the chicken to the frying pan, cover, and continue cooking for 20 minutes on a very gentle heat.

3. Remove the chicken and the figs and keep them warm.

4. Remove and discard the cinnamon.

5. Allow the sauce to boil until quite syrupy.

6. Return the chicken and the figs to the frying pan, heat through and serve.

TIME   Preparation takes about 5 minutes and cooking takes about 35 minutes.

SERVING IDEA   Serve with Rice Pilaf.

WATCHPOINT   Cook over a very gentle heat throughout Step 2, stirring from time to time to prevent sticking.

□

OPPOSITE

SLICED CHICKEN
WITH FIGS

—— SERVES 6 ——

LAPIN CHASSEUR

'Hunter's rabbit,' a delicious blend of mushrooms, smoked bacon and white wine, all cooked on top of the stove in less than an hour.

Step 1

Step 2

Step 2

Step 3

☐ 1 rabbit   ☐ 1 onion, chopped   ☐ 1 bouquet garni
☐ 1 cup white wine   ☐ 1½ cups button mushrooms, sliced
☐ ¼ lb smoked bacon, diced   ☐ 1 tbsp flour
☐ 1 tbsp butter   ☐ 1 tbsp parsley, chopped
☐ Pinch nutmeg   ☐ Salt and pepper

1. Bone the rabbit and cut the meat into small pieces.

2. Cook the bacon in a casserole on the top of the stove without adding any extra fat, until the fat from the bacon is running. Stir in the rabbit pieces, add the onions and continue cooking until the onions are tender.

3. Pour over the wine and 1 cup water. Add the bouquet garni, nutmeg, salt and pepper. Bring to the boil.

4. Cover, reduce the heat and cook for 30 minutes. Add the mushrooms and then simmer gently for a further 15 minutes.

5. Just before serving, beat together the butter and the flour. Beat this into the sauce, off of the heat, little by little until the sauce thickens to the desired consistency.

6. Serve with the parsley sprinkled over.

TIME   Preparation takes about 15 minutes and cooking takes approximately 45 minutes.

SERVING IDEA   Serve with fresh wild mushrooms gently sautéed in butter and garlic.

WATCHPOINT   When beating in the flour and butter at step 5, take care that the sauce does not thicken too much or too quickly.

☐

OPPOSITE

LAPIN CHASSEUR

SERVES 6

CHICKEN WITH TARRAGON SAUCE

Tarragon is a much used herb in the French kitchen. In this recipe, it adds its very distinctive flavor to the rich sauce.

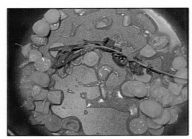

Step 2

Step 3

Step 5

□ 2 chickens, chopped into pieces   □ 6 shallots, chopped
□ 1 carrot, chopped   □ 2 tbsps fresh tarragon, chopped
□ 3 sprigs fresh tarragon   □ 3 tbsps olive oil   □ ½ cup butter
□ 1 jigger Muscat   □ ½ cup white wine
□ 1 cup chicken stock   □ Salt and pepper
□ 1 tbsp cornstarch mixed with 1 tbsp water

1. Warm the oil and half of the butter in a large casserole and brown the chicken pieces on all sides. Remove the chicken to a spare plate.

2. Add the remaining butter to the casserole and cook the shallots, carrot and the sprigs of tarragon for 5 minutes.

3. Slide the chicken pieces back into the casserole and stir well.

4. Stir in the Muscat.

5. Pour over the wine and the chicken stock, add salt and pepper, and stir well. Bring to the boil, cover, then reduce the heat and simmer for 30 minutes. Check the level of the juices and add a little water if necessary.

6. When the chicken pieces are cooked through, remove and place on a preheated serving dish.

7. Bring the sauce to the boil and allow to reduce and thicken. If necessary, stir in the cornstarch and water mixture, stirring continuously until the sauce has thickened. Serve poured over the chicken. Sprinkle over the chopped tarragon.

TIME   Preparation will take about 15 minutes and cooking takes about 40 minutes.

SERVING IDEA   Serve with sauté potatoes and garnish with sprigs of tarragon.

COOK'S TIP   If time permits, allow the sauce to reduce and thicken by itself. Only use the cornstarch if the sauce is really too thin.

□

OPPOSITE

CHICKEN WITH
TARRAGON SAUCE

———— SERVES 6 ————

POULET A L'ALSACIENNE

*This stuffed, rolled chicken is a traditional
recipe from the Alsace region.*

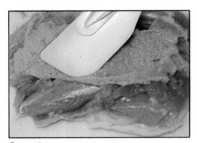

Step 2

Step 2

Step 2

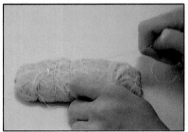

Step 2

☐ 1 large chicken, boned and cleaned (reserve the carcass, bones and liver) ☐ 1 egg, beaten ☐ 2 tbsps light cream ☐ 2 tbsps heavy cream ☐ 1 crépine (stomach bag) ☐ 1 carrot, shredded ☐ 1 leek (white part only), shredded ☐ 1 onion, shredded ☐ ¼ cup butter ☐ ½ cup white wine ☐ ¾ cup heavy cream, whipped ☐ 1 tbsp Cognac ☐ ½ cup raw foie gras (duck or goose liver) ☐ 3 tbsps oil ☐ 1 nut butter ☐ Salt and pepper

1. Remove one of the chicken breasts and, in a mixer or food processor, blend with the liver, egg, whipped cream, salt and pepper. Rub this mixture through a fine sieve and add the Cognac and 2 tbsps of heavy cream to form a stiff paste.

2. Spread this paste over the opened chicken meat and then roll up the meat neatly. Cut the crépine to fit around each piece of meat and roll up each piece neatly. If necessary, the ends can be secured by tying them up with fine kitchen string. Keep in a cool place.

3. Melt the ¼ cup butter in a heavy frying pan and cook the carrot, leek, onion and the broken up carcass and bones for 5 minutes. Pour over the white wine and cover with water. Bring to the boil and allow to cook until the sauce reduces a little and thickens slightly.

4. Strain the above through a fine sieve and then put it back in a saucepan over quite a high heat. Stir in the light cream and the remaining Cognac, and allow to reduce until quite thick.

5. Melt the nut of butter with the oil in a heavy frying pan and brown the pieces of meat on all sides. Finish cooking in a hot oven for approximately 30 minutes.

6. Just before serving the sauce, whip in the foie gras, blending with a hand mixer. Cut the meat into neat slices and pour the sauce over.

TIME   Preparation takes about 25 minutes and cooking takes 35 minutes.

COOK'S TIP   If the sauce is not very thick at the end of step 3, dissolve 1 tbsp of cornstarch with 1 tbsp water, add this to the sauce and stir continuously until the sauce thickens.

☐

OPPOSITE

POULET A
L'ALSACIENNE

————— SERVES 6 —————

QUAIL WITH GRAPES

Quail is becoming increasingly available in supermarkets, and this is an impressive yet simple dish for you to experiment with.

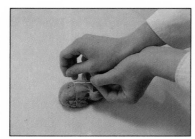

Step 1

- □ 6 quail □ ¾ lb seedless white grapes (or seeds removed)
- □ ½ cup Madeira □ 6 slices of white bread □ 2 tbsps oil
- □ ½ cup butter □ 2 cups rich chicken stock
- □ Salt and pepper

1. To prepare the birds, remove the heads and wings, then draw the quail and truss them with kitchen string.

2. Melt a nut of butter and 1 tbsp of oil in a frying pan and gently brown the birds. Remove from the pan and finish cooking in a hot oven at 400°F for approximately 15 minutes.

3. Pour off any excess fat from the pan and deglaze the pan with the Madeira. Add the grapes and then stir in the stock. Allow to reduce to a syrupy consistency.

4. Remove the grapes using a slotted spoon. Whip the remaining butter, reserving a nut for the toasts, and season with salt and pepper. Blend smooth with a hand mixer and replace the grapes.

5. Fry the toasts in the nut of butter with the remaining oil. Serve the quail on the toasts, with the sauce poured over.

TIME   Preparation takes about 20 minutes and cooking takes approximately 40 minutes.

COOK'S TIP   The grapes can be peeled, but the skins are necessary for the sauce, so add them at step 3 and then remove them just before serving.

WATCHPOINT   Drain the toasts on paper towels before serving to remove the excess fat.

□

OPPOSITE

QUAIL WITH
GRAPES

—— SERVES 6 ——

DUCK BREAST WITH GREEN PEPPERCORN SAUCE

*Duck is an ever-popular dish in France, served here
in a highly flavored, rich pepper sauce.*

Step 3

Step 5

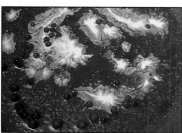

Step 5

□ 3 large duck breasts
□ 2 ¼ lbs duck or poultry bones and trimmings
□ 1 tbsp green peppercorns
□ 1 onion, finely chopped   □ 1 carrot, finely chopped
□ 1 leek, finely chopped   □ 1 cup white wine
□ 1 tbsp Cognac   □ 1 tbsp oil
□ ⅔ cup heavy cream   □ 1 tsp thyme
□ 1 bay leaf   □ Salt and pepper

1. Break up the bones and cook them in the oil in a heavy frying pan with the trimmings, 2 tbsps water, onion, carrot and leek for 5 minutes. Pour over the white wine and enough water to cover. Add salt and pepper, thyme and bay leaf, bring to the boil and allow to reduce by half.

2. When the sauce has reduced, strain it through a fine sieve, return to the heat and reduce a little more.

3. Score the skin of the duck breasts and, in a clean frying pan, seal over a high heat, skin side first. Once sealed on all sides, continue cooking in a hot oven until just a thin line of pink is visible in the center – approximately 10 to 15 minutes.

4. Set the breasts aside and keep them warm.

5. Sauté the peppercorns in the fat from the sealed duck breasts for 1 minute, add the Cognac, then stir in the reduced sauce from Step 2. Allow this to reduce a little more and then stir in the cream.

6. Cut the breasts into even slices and serve with the sauce poured over.

TIME   Preparation takes about 5 minutes and cooking takes about 40 minutes.

VARIATION   You could use duck fillets instead of breasts.

COOK'S TIP   Ask your butcher to put by the bones and trimmings a few days prior to your buying the fillets; they are essential for the rich flavoring of the sauce.

WATCHPOINT   If you prefer your meat well cooked, give the breasts a little extra time in the oven. Find out how your guests prefer their meat cooked prior to serving.

□

OPPOSITE

DUCK BREAST
WITH GREEN
PEPPERCORN
SAUCE

—— SERVES 6 ——

PERDREAUX A L'ARMAGNAC

Young, plump and tender partridges are ideal for this classic recipe. Fresh truffles are now available in specialist shops; they are expensive, but for a special meal well worth the extra cost.

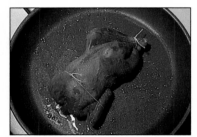

Step 1

□ 3 young partridges, cleaned, gizzards and the livers removed and retained □ 1 truffle □ ½ cup heavy cream □ 4 tbsps Armagnac □ ¼ cup butter □ 1 tbsp oil

1. Truss the birds with kitchen string. Melt ⅓ of the butter with the oil in a heavy saucepan and brown the birds on all sides. Remove them from the saucepan (retain the saucepan with the juices) and cook in a hot oven for 20 minutes.

2. Once the birds are cooked, cut off the wings, thighs and the breasts, set them aside and keep warm.

3. Crush the carcasses and put them back into the saucepan containing the juices and add the gizzards and livers. Over a high heat, pour over the Armagnac and the cream and stir well. Take off the heat and strain through a fine sieve.

4. Add the crumbled truffle, and whip in the remaining butter. Blend in a mixer or food processor until smooth.

5. Cut the partridges into slices and serve the sauce poured over.

TIME   Preparation takes about 10 minutes and cooking takes about 30 minutes.

VARIATION   If partridge is unavailable, use wood pigeon instead.

□

OPPOSITE

PERDREAUX A
L'ARMAGNAC

SERVES 6

GUINEA FOWL CASSEROLE

Guinea fowl is very popular in central France, and this recipe is easy to cook and is absolutely delicious.

Step 1

Step 2

Step 2

- □ 2 large, young guinea fowl, cleaned, dried and each cut into 4
- □ ½ lb smoked bacon, diced   □ 3 carrots, diced
- □ 2 turnips, diced   □ 1 stick celery, diced
- □ 1 onion, diced   □ 2 cups mushrooms, diced
- □ ½ cup red wine   □ 2 tbsps heavy cream
- □ ½ tbsp flour

1. Cook the bacon gently in a large casserole until the fat begins to run, then add the onion, carrots, celery and turnips. Cook until all the vegetables have turned slightly brown.

2. Using a slotted spoon, remove all the above ingredients from the casserole, and keep them on a spare plate. Put the guinea fowl pieces in the casserole, raise the heat and brown on all sides. Sprinkle over the flour, stir, and cook for 1 minute. Pour over the wine, continue stirring, then put back all the ingredients from the spare plate.

3. Stir in ¾ cup of water and the mushrooms, cover and cook in a moderately hot oven until the fowl is cooked through, stirring from time to time.

4. Stir in the cream and drain the sauce through a fine sieve. Blend the sauce with a hand mixer. Season with a little salt and pepper.

5. Serve the fowl on top of the blended sauce, covered with the mushroom and vegetable mixture.

TIME   Preparation takes about 30 minutes and cooking takes approximately 45 minutes.

TIME SAVER   Cook the casserole in advance and store in the refrigerator. To serve, heat through completely before making the sauce.

SERVING IDEA   Garnish with flat-leaved parsley and serve with lightly buttered pasta shells.

□

OPPOSITE

GUINEA FOWL
CASSEROLE

SERVES 6

PHEASANT WITH APPLES

*Pheasant, with its very distinctive flavor, is enhanced
in this recipe from Normandy by the addition of
another local product: Calvados apple brandy.*

Step 1

Step 2

Step 4

□ 1 large pheasant, wiped and cut into 6 pieces
□ 2 thick strips smoked bacon
□ 5 cooking apples, peeled and sliced
□ 1 onion, finely chopped   □ ¾ cup heavy cream
□ 3 tbsps Calvados   □ 2 tbsps oil
□ 2 tbsps butter   □ Salt and pepper

1. Melt the butter with the oil in a large frying pan and cook the bacon and the onion. Remove with a slotted spoon when tender, and keep on a spare plate.

2. Brown the pheasant pieces in the same frying pan. Remove and keep on the spare plate once they are nicely colored and sealed.

3. Add the sliced apple to the same pan, season with salt and pepper and cook until nicely browned. Put the cooked apple on the spare plate. Now wipe out the frying pan with paper towels.

4. Put all the above cooked ingredients back into the clean frying pan, pour over the Calvados and ½ cup water, cover and cook over a gentle heat for 10 minutes.

5. Pour all the contents of the frying pan into a casserole, cover and finish cooking in a moderately hot oven for 15 minutes. Stir in the cream halfway through cooking.

6. Take the casserole out of the oven and remove the pheasant. Allow the sauce to reduce somewhat over a fairly high heat, then blend smooth in a blender. Put the sauce and pheasant pieces back into the casserole. Taste and adjust the seasoning if necessary, and serve immediately.

TIME   Preparation takes about 10 minutes and cooking time is approximately 45 to 50 minutes.

WATCHPOINT   The sauce in this recipe needs no thickening agent as the cooked apples are a natural thickener.

□

OPPOSITE

PHEASANT WITH
APPLES

——— SERVES 6 ———

FILLET OF LAMB WITH FRESH THYME SAUCE

A delicately flavored sauce to go with tender spring lamb, filleted from the saddle.

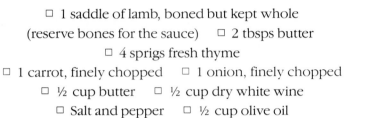

☐ 1 saddle of lamb, boned but kept whole
(reserve bones for the sauce)   ☐ 2 tbsps butter
☐ 4 sprigs fresh thyme
☐ 1 carrot, finely chopped   ☐ 1 onion, finely chopped
☐ ½ cup butter   ☐ ½ cup dry white wine
☐ Salt and pepper   ☐ ½ cup olive oil

1. Heat half of the olive oil and sauté the broken bones with the carrot and onion. Wipe out any excess fat, deglaze the frying pan with the wine, cover the ingredients with water and leave at a gentle boil for 1 hour.

2. Strain the juices through a very fine sieve into a clean saucepan. Put onto a high heat, add the thyme, and allow to reduce until quite thick.

3. Melt 2 tbsps butter and the remaining oil in the frying pan and seal the lamb on all sides. Finish cooking the lamb in a hot oven for 15 minutes.

4. Just before serving, strain the reduced juices through a fine sieve to eliminate the thyme. Mix the remaining ½ cup butter into the sauce, and blend smooth with a hand mixer. Cut the lamb into slices and serve.

TIME   Preparation will take about 10 minutes, longer if you are boning the meat yourself. Cooking takes approximately 1 hour and 30 minutes.

SERVING IDEA   Serve with a Gratin Dauphinois.

COOK'S TIP   If the rolled fillet is very thick and you like your lamb well cooked, cook the lamb for longer in the oven at the end of Step 3.

☐

OPPOSITE

FILLET OF LAMB
WITH FRESH
THYME SAUCE

PETIT SALE AUX LENTILLES

*Petit salé literally means small and salty. This recipe
is in fact a ham cut cooked with green lentils.*

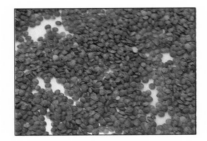

Step 3

Step 3

☐ 2lbs green lentils   ☐ 2½ lbs ham   ☐ 6 herb sausages
☐ ½ lb carrots, cut into chunks
☐ 1 large onion, stuck with 2 whole cloves
☐ 1 bouquet garni   ☐ Salt and pepper

---

1. Wash the ham under running water, place it in a large saucepan and cover with cold water. Bring to the boil, reduce heat and cook for 2 hours.

2. After 2 hours, add the sausages to the saucepan, cook for 10 minutes and then remove from the heat.

3. Set the lentils to cook in a large quantity of water with the onion, carrot bouquet garni and a little salt. Bring gently to the boil, reduce the heat and simmer for approximately 30 to 40 minutes.

4. After about 30 minutes, add the ham and the sausages and continue cooking until the lentils are cooked.

5. Drain off a little of the liquid, if necessary, and remove the bouquet garni. Cut the meat and the sausages into chunks, put back into the saucepan, heat through again and serve.

TIME   Preparation takes about 20 minutes and cooking takes almost 3 hours.

SERVING IDEA   Cut the ham into small chunks and the sausages into small rounds, this will make the finished dish much more attractive.

WATCHPOINT   Green lentils cook quite quickly and their skins are fragile, so they must be cooked on a gentle simmer and not a rapid boil.

☐

OPPOSITE

PETIT SALE AUX
LENTILLES

CALF'S LIVER
WITH ORANGE SAUCE

*Serve this delicious recipe with confidence for your most
elegant dinner parties; it's sure to be a great success.*

Step 1

Step 2

☐ 1 large piece of calf's liver, cut into slices
☐ 4 oranges (2 squeezed for their juice, and the remaining
2 peeled and cut into thin slices)
☐ 1 cup veal stock   ☐ ⅔ cup butter
☐ Salt and pepper   ☐ 1 tbsp chopped chives

1. Heat ¾ of the butter in a frying pan and cook the liver briskly on both sides. Remove the liver and keep warm on a plate over a saucepan of boiling water.

2. Wipe out the excess fat, deglaze the pan with the juice of 2 oranges and scrape the bottom of the pan with a wooden spoon to mix any remaining liver into the juice. Add the veal stock, salt and pepper, bring to the boil and add the orange slices.

3. Allow to color slightly, remove the slices with a fork and place them on the liver.

4. Remove the pan from the heat and stir in the remaining butter.

5. Serve the sauce poured over the liver and sliced oranges. Garnish with the chopped chives.

TIME   Preparation takes about 8 minutes and cooking takes approximately 25 to 30 minutes.

SERVING IDEA   Serve with boiled or steamed new potatoes.

VARIATION   Replace 2 of the oranges with a large grapefruit. Cut it in half, squeeze the juice from one half and peel and slice the remaining half. Divide 2 oranges in the same way.

☐

OPPOSITE

CALF'S LIVER WITH
ORANGE SAUCE

─────── SERVES 4 ───────

STEAMED CALVES' LIVER

A richly flavored sauce with fresh tarragon enhances the calves'
liver delightfully; the liver should be served slightly pink.

Step 1

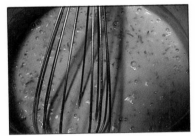
Step 4

☐ 2 ¼ lbs calves' liver   ☐ 1 sprig fresh tarragon
☐ 2 shallots, chopped   ☐ 1 tsp peppercorns, lightly crushed
☐ 6 tbsps vinegar   ☐ 1 cup whipping cream, whipped
☐ 6 tbsps butter   ☐ 6 tbsps milk   ☐ Salt and pepper

1. Chop half of the tarragon finely, and put it into a saucepan with the vinegar, shallots and peppercorns. Heat, and allow to boil until the vinegar has almost completely evaporated, then whip in the cream and the milk. Allow to reduce and then strain through a fine sieve. Remove from the heat, but keep warm.

2. Steam the liver on a bed of the remaining tarragon until still just pink in the center. Sprinkle with salt and pepper.

3. Slice the liver thinly and serve on a pre-heated plate.

4. Put the sauce back onto a gentle heat and whisk in the butter. Serve the sauce immediately.

TIME   Preparation takes about 5 minutes, and cooking takes 40 minutes.

WATCHPOINT   Serve the sauce immediately and do not try to reheat it once the butter has been added.

COOK'S TIP   Find out in advance how guests prefer their liver cooked.

WATCHPOINT   Be careful when reducing the sauce during Step 1; it thickens very quickly, and you must remove the sauce from the heat before it becomes too thick.

☐

OPPOSITE

STEAMED CALVES'
LIVER

SERVES 6

CASSOULET

*A classic casserole, served throughout France. Great
for cold winter evenings in front of a roaring fire.*

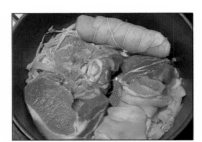
Step 1

Step 1

Step 2

Step 2

□

OPPOSITE

CASSOULET

- □ 6 cups lima beans, presoaked (12 hours)   □ 1 onion
- □ 2 whole cloves   □ 1 leek, cut into chunks
- □ 1 carrot, cut into chunks   □ 1½ lbs pork loin
- □ ½ cup goose or other poultry dripping
- □ 2 cloves garlic, chopped   □ 1 pork knuckle
- □ ¾ lb bacon, whole   □ ½ shoulder lamb
- ½ lb herb sausages   □ 4 tomatoes, halved   □ 1 bouquet garni
- □ 1 tsp thyme   □ 1 bay leaf   □ Salt and pepper

1. In a large flameproof casserole, melt the dripping and seal the pork knuckle and the loin. Then add the onion, garlic, leek, tomatoes, carrot, bay leaf and the bouquet garni. Stir well and cook for a few minutes.

2. Add the drained beans, and enough water to cover the contents of the casserole. Bring to the boil then reduce the heat, cover and simmer for 2 hours on a very gentle heat. After about one hour, add the sausages, bacon, and the shoulder of lamb. Check the water level during cooking and add water when necessary.

3. After the full 2 hours, strain off the juice into a clean saucepan and chop the meat into bite-sized pieces. Discard most of the bones.

4. Remove the bay leaf and the bouquet garni.

5. In a large earthenware bowl, place layers of the chopped meats, beans and sausages. Pour over 2 to 3 cups of the cooking juice, cover and continue cooking in a hot oven for 35 minutes.

6. Serve piping hot from the oven.

TIME   Preparation takes about 20 minutes and cooking takes approximately 3 hours.

COOK'S TIP   Cassoulet is even better if cooked the day before and reheated just before serving. Make sure that there is enough liquid in the casserole, adding water as necessary.

SERVING IDEA   Simply serve plenty of French stick with this substantial main course.

SERVES 6

KIDNEY FRICASSEE

Sautéed calf's kidney in a sweet, creamy sauce.

- □ 2lbs calf's kidney   □ 1½ cups mushrooms, sliced
- □ 2 tbsps Madeira   □ ½ cup veal stock
- □ ¼ cup heavy cream   □ 1 tbsp olive oil   □ Salt and pepper

1. Prepare the kidney by cutting it into small cubes. Heat the oil in a frying pan and sauté the kidney and the mushrooms. Season with salt and pepper. Remove the kidney and keep it warm.

2. Deglaze the frying pan with the Madeira and allow the liquid to reduce a little. Stir in the stock and reduce by half.

3. Stir in the cream and add the salt and pepper. Put the kidney back into the sauce and heat through. Serve hot.

TIME   Preparation takes about 15 minutes and cooking takes approximately 30 minutes.

COOK'S TIP   You will notice that the cooked kidney loses a lot of blood once you have removed it from the frying pan. Allow this blood to drain off – do not add it to the sauce.

□

OPPOSITE

KIDNEY FRICASSEE

SAUTE D'AGNEAU

A quick and easy recipe consisting of tender lamb in red wine and mushroom sauce, all done on the top of a stove.

Step 1

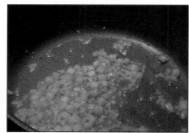

Step 2

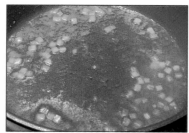

Step 3

Step 4

□ 2 ¼ lbs shoulder of lamb, cut into chunks
□ 2 tbsps olive oil   □ 3 sticks celery, cut into small cubes
□ 1 onion, finely chopped   □ ½ cup red wine
□ ½ cup beef stock
□ 2 tbsps cornstarch mixed with 2 tbsps water
□ 1 tbsp tomato paste
□ 1½ cups mushrooms, washed, wiped and sliced
□ Salt and pepper

1. Warm half the olive oil in a frying pan and seal the pieces of lamb on all sides. Allow to brown slightly, then remove from the heat and keep warm.

2. Add the remaining oil and sauté the celery, onion and mushrooms.

3. Stirring constantly, add the wine, stock, tomato paste and the dissolved cornstarch. Stir until the sauce thickens.

4. Put the lamb back in the frying pan with the above ingredients, add a little salt and pepper, cover and cook for a further 15 to 25 minutes.

5. Remove the lamb and blend the sauce in a blender until smooth. Serve the meat with the sauce poured over.

TIME   Preparation takes about 5 minutes and cooking time is approximately 40 minutes.

ECONOMY   Remove a few pieces of celery before blending the sauce; these will serve as a ready-made garnish.

SERVING IDEA   Serve with boiled or steamed new potatoes.

□

OPPOSITE

SAUTE D'AGNEAU

SERVES 6

ROAST PORK WITH GARLIC CREAM

A distinctively-flavored sauce enhances the roast pork marvelously in a dish that is definitely for garlic lovers.

Step 1

Step 1

☐ 2 ¼ lb pork roast   ☐ 1 head garlic, all the cloves peeled
☐ 1 cup light cream, whipped   ☐ 2 tbsps oil   ☐ ⅓ cup port
☐ 1 nut butter   ☐ Salt and pepper

1. Trim off any excess fat or gristle from the meat, setting the trimmings aside for use in the sauce, roll the meat into a roast and secure with string.

2. Sauté the meat trimmings in half of the oil with the garlic, and allow to brown slightly. Pour off the excess fat from the pan and stir in the port. Remove from the heat and stir in the cream.

3. Remove a few cloves of garlic for decoration. Blend the sauce smooth with a hand mixer and then strain through a fine sieve.

4. Put the sauce back on the heat and allow to reduce a little. Remove from the heat and keep it warm.

5. Warm the remaining oil in a large frying pan and seal the roast on all sides. Finish cooking in a moderately hot oven for 20 to 40 minutes depending on the thickness of the roast.

6. Slice the roast and serve on a pre-heated plate with the sauce poured over and the few cloves of garlic as decoration.

TIME   Preparation will take about 15 minutes and cooking takes about 1 hour.

SERVING IDEA   Serve with a colorful vegetable such as carrot or broccoli.

COOK'S TIP   When sealing the meat, allow it to brown nicely, making the finished dish even more appetizing.

WATCHPOINT   To help keep the meat moist, wrap the roast in aluminum foil halfway through the oven cooking time.

☐

OPPOSITE

ROAST PORK WITH GARLIC CREAM

—— SERVES 6 ——

PAUPIETTES DE VEAU

Veal paupiettes or birds are a delicious way of serving this lean, delicate and distinctive tasting meat.

- ☐ 6 very thin slices of veal, each weighing approximately 4oz
- ☐ 6oz shoulder veal ☐ 1 egg ☐ ¼ cup butter
- ☐ 4 sprigs parsley ☐ 3 shallots, finely chopped
- ☐ 2 onions, finely chopped ☐ 4 tomatoes, halved
- ☐ 3 button mushrooms ☐ Bouquet garni ☐ 1 jigger port
- ☐ ½ cup heavy cream ☐ Salt and pepper

Step 3

Step 3

Step 3

1. Trim the slices of veal into even-sized rectangles. Keep the veal in a cool place whilst making the stuffing.

2. Grind the trimmings, shoulder of veal, parsley, mushrooms, salt and pepper together in a food processor.

3. Beat the egg with 1 tbsp cream and mix this egg mixture and the ground meat together well. Place the stuffing on the slices of veal and roll them up into neat oblongs. Tie with kitchen string.

4. Melt half of the butter in a frying pan and seal the veal on all sides until nicely browned. Continue cooking for approximately 10 minutes.

5. Pour over the port, stir, and add the tomatoes, shallots, bouquet garni and a little more pepper. Cover, and leave to simmer gently for 30 minutes.

6. To serve, place the paupiettes on a pre-heated serving dish. Remove the bouquet garni from the sauce, stir the remaining cream into the sauce and pour over the paupiettes. If you prefer a smooth sauce, strain it through a fine sieve and then blend smooth with a hand mixer.

TIME   Preparation takes about 30 minutes and cooking takes approximately 50 minutes.

SERVING IDEA   Remove the string from the paupiettes and cut each one into slices.

GARNISH   Garnish the dish with a little chopped carrot and parsley.

WATCHPOINT   Do not allow the sauce to boil once you have stirred in the remaining cream.

☐

OPPOSITE

PAUPIETTES DE VEAU

—— SERVES 4-6 ——

HONEYED SPARE RIBS

*Lovely sweet-sour finger food, great
for a picnic or a family meal.*

Step 1

☐ 3 ½ lbs spare ribs   ☐ 2 tbsps honey   ☐ 1 sprig thyme
☐ 2 tbsps Xeres vinegar   ☐ 1 clove garlic, chopped
☐ 1 carrot, halved   ☐ 1 leek, halved   ☐ 1 onion, halved
☐ 1 bay leaf   ☐ 1 tbsp oil   ☐ Salt and pepper

1. Boil the onion, leek, bay leaf and carrot in salted water. Once the water is boiling, plunge the spare ribs in until it comes to the boil again, then remove them with a slotted spoon. Drain well and separate the ribs.

2. Warm the oil in a large frying pan, add the garlic and then the ribs. Seal the ribs over a high heat, then reduce the heat and cook for 1 minute.

3. Deglaze the frying pan with the vinegar, stir in the honey and 3 tbsps water and add the thyme. Season with salt and pepper.

4. Transfer to an ovenproof dish and cook in a moderately hot oven until the ribs are caramelized. Turn the ribs frequently during cooking.

5. Serve either hot or cold, with the juices poured around the plate.

TIME   Preparation takes about 10 minutes and cooking takes approximately 30 minutes.

SERVING IDEA   The ribs go well with a salad and a garlic vinaigrette.

☐

OPPOSITE

HONEYED
SPARE RIBS

SERVES 6

ROAST LEG OF LAMB

The addition of garlic to the roast lends a very subtle flavor.
Lamb is a great favorite in Central France.

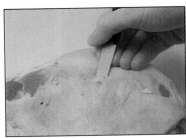

Step 2

Step 2

☐ 1 leg lamb (approx. 4½ lbs)　☐ 2 cloves garlic, halved
☐ 2 tbsps olive oil　☐ Salt and pepper
☐ 4 tbsps water

1. Preheat the oven to 400°F.

2. Make 4 cuts in the leg of lamb with the end of a sharp knife, and push a piece of garlic into each.

3. Place the lamb in a roasting pan with the 4 tbsps water, pour over the olive oil, and sprinkle with salt and pepper.

4. Cook for 1 to 1½ hours, turning the leg halfway through the cooking time.

5. Serve on a carving dish, with the juices in a sauce boat.

TIME　Preparation takes under 5 minutes and cooking takes approximately 1½ hours.

SERVING IDEA　Serve with crisp, fresh vegetables.

WATCHPOINT　The leg may need to be covered with aluminum foil during cooking if the top begins to burn.

COOK'S TIP　A little more water added to the roasting pan helps to keep the meat moist.

PREPARATION　Ask your butcher to remove the bone, but replace it during cooking. This will make it easier to carve.

☐

OPPOSITE

ROAST LEG OF
LAMB

—————— SERVES 6 ——————

MIGNON DE PORC AU CHOU

Pork fillet, roasted with cabbage and bacon.

Step 1

Step 2

Step 4

☐ 2 ¼ lbs pork fillet, cut in two   ☐ ½ lb smoked bacon, chopped
☐ ½ cup drippings   ☐ 2 ¼ lbs green cabbage, shredded
☐ 1 cup chicken stock   ☐ Salt and pepper

1. Remove any gristle from the meat and cut off any excess fat. Roll up the roasts and tie them securely with kitchen string.

2. Bring to the boil a large quantity of lightly salted water and blanch the shredded cabbage for 2 minutes. Drain well, squeezing out excess water.

3. Melt the drippings in a large frying pan and seal the pork on all sides. Allow the meat to brown slightly, then remove the roasts and keep them warm.

4. Add the bacon and cabbage to the frying pan, stir well, and cook for 4 minutes.

5. Transfer the contents to a casserole, add the roasts and the stock, and finish cooking in a moderately hot oven for approximately 40 minutes.

6. Turn the cabbage, juices and roasts from time to time in the oven. When cooked, cut the roasts into slices and serve hot.

TIME   Preparation takes about 15 minutes and cooking takes approximately 1 hour.

WATCHPOINT   When turning the contents of the casserole, make sure that the meat is well covered with the juice and cabbage otherwise it will be too dry. Add a little more stock if the liquid evaporates too quickly.

SERVING IDEA   Serve with roast potatoes.

VARIATION   Use pork chops instead of fillet.

☐

OPPOSITE

MIGNON DE PORC
AU CHOU

CARRE D'AGNEAU A LA PROVENÇALE

Herbes de Provence, a mixture of dried herbs with a dominance of thyme, give this rack of lamb recipe from the South of France a distinctive flavor.

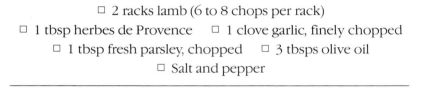

□ 2 racks lamb (6 to 8 chops per rack)
□ 1 tbsp herbes de Provence   □ 1 clove garlic, finely chopped
□ 1 tbsp fresh parsley, chopped   □ 3 tbsps olive oil
□ Salt and pepper

1. Begin the night before by preparing the oil. In a large screw-top jar, mix together the oil, parsley, garlic, herbs, salt and lots of pepper. Shake well.

2. Make small incisions all over the lamb and pour over the oil, basting the meat with the oil several times.

3. The next day, preheat the oven to 400°F and cook the lamb for approximately 15 minutes, slightly longer if you prefer your meat a little less pink.

TIME   Preparation takes about 5 minutes, with overnight mixing for the oil, and about 20 to 30 minutes cooking.

SERVING IDEA   Serve with Haricots Verts a la Provençale.

COOK'S TIP   Choose a rack of lamb with long, thin chops, as this will cook more quickly.

□

OPPOSITE

CARRE D'AGNEAU A
LA PROVENÇALE

— SERVES 6 —

OLD FASHIONED BEEF CASSEROLE

This traditional recipe from the east of France incorporates overnight marinating – the secret of a very tender beef casserole.

Step 1

□ 2 ¼ lbs best braising beef   □ 2 tbsps oil   □ 1 carrot, sliced
□ 2 large onions, sliced   □ 2 cups red wine
□ 2 tomatoes, peeled, halved, seeded and crushed
□ 1 cup mushrooms, wiped and sliced
□ 20 small onions, peeled   □ 1 bouquet garni
□ 1 clove garlic, chopped   □ Salt and pepper
□ Chives for garnish

1.   Begin the day before by cutting the beef into small cubes. To make the marinade, mix together the wine, oil, sliced onions, carrot, bouquet garni and the garlic, stirring well. Add the beef, coating it thoroughly in the mixture. Cover, and leave to marinate in a cool place, stirring from time to time.

2.   The next day, put the beef with its marinade into a casserole dish together with the tomatoes, adding a little salt and pepper. Bring to the boil, then reduce the heat and simmer for 2 hours in a preheated 300°F oven.

3.   After 2 hours, add the baby onions and the mushrooms. Continue cooking for 30 minutes.

4.   Remove the slices of onion and the bouquet garni. Serve hot, garnished with a few chive leaves.

TIME   Preparation will take about 10 minutes, plus overnight marinating, and cooking takes 2 ½ hours.

SERVING IDEA   Serve with a brightly colored vegetable, such as Pois Bonne Femme, or with lightly buttered pasta.

TIME SAVER   Cook the casserole in advance and warm it through thoroughly before serving.

□

OPPOSITE

OLD FASHIONED
BEEF CASSEROLE

—— SERVES 6 ——

FILET D'AGNEAU EN CROUTE

Lamb fillets covered with puff pastry and served with a light wine and garlic sauce.

Step 1

Step 3

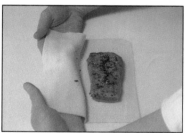

Step 3

Step 3

□

OPPOSITE

FILET D'AGNEAU EN CROUTE

- □ 2 lamb fillets, cut from the shoulder or leg (reserve a few bones for the sauce)
- □ 1½ cups prepared puff paste dough
- □ 2 tbsps fresh parsley, chopped
- □ 1 clove garlic, chopped   □ Salt and pepper
- □ 6 tbsps butter   □ 1 cup white wine
- □ 1 carrot, finely chopped   □ 1 onion, finely chopped
- □ 1 sprig thyme   □ 1 bay leaf
- □ 1 tbsp olive oil   □ 1 egg, beaten

1. Prepare the fillets, removing and retaining any fat or gristle for the sauce. Lightly pepper the meat. Warm the oil and a nut of butter in a frying pan, and seal the meat on all sides. Remove the meat and keep warm.

2. Sauté in the frying pan the trimmings, bones, carrot, onion, thyme, and the bay leaf. Wipe out the excess fat and deglaze the pan with the white wine. Cover with water, bring to the boil, skim off any fat which rises, and leave to reduce and thicken.

3. Roll the pastry very thinly into 2 rectangles. Place the fillets onto the pastry, sprinkle over the chopped garlic and parsley, fold the pastry round the fillets and seal the edges with the beaten egg. Brush a little beaten egg over the top and cook in a hot oven for approximately 15 minutes.

4. Strain the thickened sauce through a fine sieve, return to the heat and allow to reduce a little and thicken. Stir in the remaining butter.

5. Cut the encased fillet into slices and serve with the sauce.

TIME   Preparation takes about 15 minutes and cooking takes approximately 45 minutes.

VARIATION   Pâté brisée may be used instead of the puff pastry.

WATCHPOINT   Check that the pastry does not begin to catch and burn during cooking. If this should happen cover the top with aluminum foil.

SERVES 6

PORK FILLETS WITH PRUNES

*An easy meal to prepare and cook, with
a delicious, slightly sweet sauce.*

Step 2

Step 2

Step 2

☐ 2 ¼ lbs pork fillet ☐ 20 strips smoked bacon
☐ 1½ cups pitted prunes ☐ 1 shallot, finely chopped
☐ ½ carrot, finely chopped ☐ 1 tbsp olive oil
☐ 2 tbsps port ☐ 1 cup chicken stock ☐ Salt and pepper

1. Remove any fat or gristle from the meat.

2. Cut the meat into steaks, roll a strip of bacon around each steak and secure with kitchen string.

3. Heat the olive oil in a frying pan and seal the steaks on all sides.

4. Put the steaks in a moderately hot oven and cook for approximately 20 minutes. Cooking time will depend on the thickness of the meat and individual taste.

5. Wipe out the excess oil from the frying pan and gently cook the onion and carrot. Increase heat, add the port and then the stock. Bring to the boil and allow to reduce by about a third.

6. Pour the sauce into a blender and blend, adding ¾ of the pitted prunes, a few at a time, until the mixture is smooth. Return the sauce to the heat and warm through.

7. Serve the steaks on the sauce, and decorate with the remaining whole prunes.

TIME   Preparation will take about 20 minutes and cooking takes approximately 40 minutes.

WATCHPOINT   Do not allow the sauce to reduce too much; if it is too thick, stir in a little water.

FREEZER   This sauce can be made in advance and stored in the freezer until required.

☐

OPPOSITE

PORK FILLETS
WITH PRUNES

SERVES 6

ESTOUFFADE DE BOEUF

*A rich beef casserole with olives and mushrooms
– perfect as a warming winter dinner.*

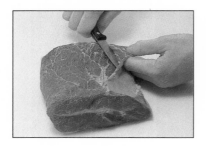

□ 2 ¼ lbs best braising steak, cut into smallish chunks
□ ½ lb smoked bacon, cubed   □ 4 onions, sliced
□ 2 cloves garlic, chopped   □ 1 bottle red wine
□ 1 cup mushrooms, sliced   □ ½ cup pitted black olives
□ 2 tbsps olive oil   □ 2 tbsps all-purpose flour
□ 1 bouquet garni (with lots of thyme)   □ Salt and pepper

1. Heat 1 tbsp olive oil in a large, flame-proof casserole and cook the bacon until the juices run.

2. Roll the meat in the flour and shake off the excess. Add the meat to the casserole with the bacon and the onions, and seal the meat on all sides. Wipe out the excess fat.

3. Add salt and pepper and pour over the wine. Stir well, then allow to reduce over a high heat, until about half of the liquid remains.

4. Add the bouquet garni and the garlic, cover and cook in a moderate oven for 2 hours, checking and stirring from time to time.

5. Sauté the mushrooms in the remaining olive oil.

6. Strain the contents of the casserole through a sieve, catching the juices in a clean saucepan. Put the meat and onions back into the casserole and add the sautéed mushrooms.

7. Put the juices back on the heat, skim off any rising fat, then stir in the olives.

8. Pour this sauce back over the contents of the casserole and cook for a further 20 minutes. Remove the bouquet garni. Serve hot.

TIME   Preparation will take about 10 minutes and cooking takes approximately 1 hour and 40 minutes.

COOK'S TIP   The estouffade is even more delicious if reheated and served the following day.

SERVING IDEA   Serve with boiled or steamed new potatoes.

WINE TIP   Serve the same wine as you have used in the cooking of the dish.

□

OPPOSITE

ESTOUFFADE
DE BOEUF

—— SERVES 6 ——

BEEF BOURGUIGNON

*A great French classic, this traditional beef casserole
should be cooked using a very good claret to give it
its extremely rich flavor.*

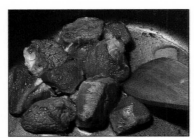
Step 2

Step 2

Step 2

☐ 4 ½ lbs braising steak, cut into cubes
☐ 6 strips smoked bacon, cut into small pieces
☐ 20 baby onions, peeled
☐ 2 tbsps flour   ☐ 1 tbsp oil
☐ A bottle of red wine   ☐ Salt and pepper

1. In a large saucepan, cook the bacon and the onions without adding any extra fat. Remove with a slotted spoon once they begin to brown.

2. Add the oil and seal the cubes of meat on all sides. Sprinkle over the flour, allow it to brown slightly and pour over the wine, stirring well. Add water to cover only if necessary. Add salt and pepper and bring to the boil.

3. Reduce the heat and replace the onions and the bacon from Step 1. Cover and simmer for 2 hours.

4. Serve hot.

TIME   Preparation takes about 5 minutes and cooking takes 2 hours and 10 minutes.

SERVING IDEA   Delicious with boiled baby carrots and new potatoes. Serve with a bottle of the same wine used for cooking.

COOK'S TIP   Simmer on a very, very gentle heat for at least 2 hours. Watch the level of the juices and add a little water, if necessary, during cooking.

☐

OPPOSITE

BEEF
BOURGUIGNON

TOURNEDOS MAITRE D'HOTEL

*Tender tournedos steaks cut from the most tender
fillet steak available, served with herb butter.*

Step 1

Step 2

Step 3

□ 6 tournedos steaks   □ ½ cup butter, softened at room
temperature   □ 2 tbsps fresh herbs, chopped
□ 1 tsp lemon juice   □ Salt and pepper

1. Beat the butter in a bowl until quite soft. Add the herbs and beat well.

2. Beat in the lemon juice and a little salt and pepper.

3. Place the butter on a sheet of aluminum foil and roll it into an oblong. Put the butter in the freezer.

4. Cook the steaks under a hot broiler and serve on a serving dish with the cold butter cut into slices.

TIME   The butter takes about 10 minutes to prepare and the steaks cook in 7 to 12 minutes, depending on thickness and personal preference.

COOK'S TIP   Cut the cold butter with a sharp, wet knife.

VARIATION   Make different flavored butters by using different herbs such as chives or parsley.

□

OPPOSITE

**TOURNEDOS
MAITRE D'HOTEL**

HUNTER'S TOURNEDOS STEAKS

*A lovely rich tasting sauce made with cognac and
white wine and left to reduce and thicken.*

Step 2

Step 3

□ 6 tournedos steaks   □ 1½ cups button mushrooms, sliced
□ ¼ cup shallots, chopped   □ 3 tbsps Cognac
□ 7 tbsps white wine   □ 1 cup beef stock   □ 4 tbsps butter
□ 1 tbsp fresh tarragon, chopped   □ Salt and pepper

---

1. Melt ⅓ of the butter in a frying pan and cook the mushrooms, tarragon and shallots until tender.

2. Deglaze the pan with the Cognac. Stir in the wine and the stock. Season well.

3. Allow this sauce to reduce until quite thick and syrupy.

4. Cook the steaks to your liking under a hot broiler.

5. Whisk the remaining butter into the sauce and serve poured over the steaks.

TIME   Preparation takes about 8 minutes and cooking takes approximately 25 minutes.

SERVING IDEA   Serve with fresh sautéed mushrooms.

COOK'S TIP   Use dried tarragon if fresh is unavailable.

□

OPPOSITE

HUNTER'S
TOURNEDOS
STEAKS

───── SERVES 6 ─────

BOEUF EN DAUBE

Quite simply a beef stew, but with those little French touches that make a world of difference.

□ 2 ¼ lbs chuck beef   □ ½ lb smoked bacon, diced
□ 4 sprigs parsley   □ 4 cloves garlic, chopped
□ 2 onions, chopped   □ 2 carrots, chopped
□ 1 bottle red wine   □ 2 tbsps olive oil   □ Salt and pepper

Step 2

1. Remove any excess fat from the meat and cut into quite large cubes.

2. Slice the cubes open on one side and place a little bacon, parsley, garlic, salt and pepper in each slice.

Step 2

3. Close each cube of meat and secure with a wooden pick.

4. Warm the olive oil in a frying pan and seal the meat on all sides. Remove the wooden picks.

5. Empty the contents of the pan into a flameproof casserole, add the onion and carrot, and pour over the wine. Bring to the boil and allow the liquid to reduce a little.

Step 2

6. Cover and continue cooking on a gentle heat for 3 hours. Check the level of the juices from time to time, stirring, and add water if necessary.

TIME   Preparation takes about 20 minutes and cooking takes at least 4 hours.

COOK'S TIP   Should the sauce be to liquid once the casserole is cooked, mix 1 tbsp cornstarch with 1 tbsp water and add this to the sauce, stirring continuously while the sauce thickens.

TIME SAVER   If you are short of time, it is not absolutely necessary to roll up the meat around the bacon, parsley and garlic, although doing so will improve presentation and ensure that the flavors are sealed in.

□

OPPOSITE

BOEUF EN DAUBE

—— SERVES 4-5 ——

BLANQUETTE DE VEAU

Cubes of veal served in a smooth blanquette sauce.
Blanquette indicates a sauce which has been prepared
using a roux (a mixture of equal parts of flour and butter).

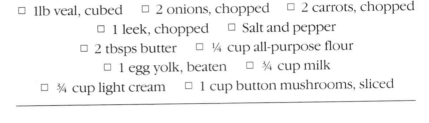

☐ 1lb veal, cubed   ☐ 2 onions, chopped   ☐ 2 carrots, chopped
☐ 1 leek, chopped   ☐ Salt and pepper
☐ 2 tbsps butter   ☐ ¼ cup all-purpose flour
☐ 1 egg yolk, beaten   ☐ ¾ cup milk
☐ ¾ cup light cream   ☐ 1 cup button mushrooms, sliced

1. Put the cubes of meat into a large flameproof casserole, cover with cold water and bring to the boil. Add the onions, leek, carrots, salt and pepper.

2. Bring to the boil once again, then reduce the heat and cover. Cook until the meat is tender, skimming off the fat that rises to the surface from time to time.

3. Remove the cooked meat with a slotted spoon, and keep the meat warm.

4. In a small saucepan, melt the butter and stir in the flour. Stir this roux into the juices in the casserole, adding the roux, little by little, until the sauce thickens. Add the mushrooms. Reduce the heat and cook for 15 minutes, stirring regularly.

5. Beat the milk and the cream into the egg yolk, and beat half of this mixture into the casserole. Once it is well incorporated, beat in the remaining mixture, beating continuously to avoid curdling.

6. Add the meat, heat through and serve on a preheated serving dish.

TIME   Preparation takes about 10 minutes and cooking takes approximately 45 minutes.

SERVING IDEA   This dish is traditionally served with boiled, long grain rice.

VARIATION   Just before serving, 2 tbsps heavy cream can be stirred into the sauce to add more richness.

☐

OPPOSITE

BLANQUETTE
DE VEAU

SIRLOIN STEAK WITH CIDER SAUCE

A recipe from Normandy which features both apples and cider.

Step 4

Step 4

□ 1 piece sirloin steak (approximately 2 ¼ lbs)
□ 1 shallot, chopped   □ 2 cups dry cider
□ 1 apple, peeled, cored and sliced   □ 1 cup beef stock
□ 2 tbsps oil   □ ¼ cup butter   □ 1 nut butter

1. Melt the nut of butter in a frying pan with the oil, and cook the shallot and the apple slices until tender.

2. Pour over the cider, increase the heat and allow the juices to reduce.

3. Pour over the stock and allow to reduce once again – not too much as the apples will make the sauce quite thick. Push the contents of the pan through a fine sieve and blend smooth with a hand mixer.

4. Cook the steak to your liking in a frying pan, then carve into slices. Serve on a preheated serving dish.

5. Return the sauce to the heat and whisk in the ¼ cup butter.

6. Serve with the sauce poured over the steak.

TIME   Preparation takes about 5 minutes and cooking takes approximately 35 minutes.

SERVING IDEA   Serve with Pommes Dauphinois.

COOK'S TIP   Once the meat is cooked, wrap quickly in aluminum foil; this helps to keep the blood in the center.

VARIATION   The meat can be cooked under a hot broiler and then cut into slices.

□

OPPOSITE

SIRLOIN STEAK
WITH CIDER SAUCE

--------- SERVES 4-6 ---------

FRUIT SORBETS

Real fruit sorbets are a delicious way of finishing off meals on hot summer evenings.

Step 3

Step 4

SORBET A L'ORANGE

☐ 1 cup fresh orange juice   ☐ ⅓ cup fresh lemon juice
☐ Zest of 1 orange   ☐ 1 heaped cup sugar

1. Dissolve the sugar in 2 cups water, bring to the boil and boil continuously for 10 minutes. Set aside to cool.

2. Blanch the orange zest in boiling water.

3. Mix the cooled syrup with the orange and lemon juice, and stir in the zest. Pour the mixture into a plastic container and place in the freezer.

4. Remove the sorbet from the freezer every 30 minutes and beat with a fork until it has completely crystallized.

TIME   Preparation takes about 5 minutes, blanching the zest about 2 minutes and freezing about 3 to 4 hours.

SERVING IDEA   Cut seasonal fruits into slices and spread out into fan shapes, serving balls of sorbet on top of the fruit.

PEAR SORBET

☐ 1lb pears, peeled and chopped   ☐ 5 tbsps sugar
☐ 3 tbsps lemon juice
☐ 1 egg white and a pinch salt, whipped until stiff

1. Dissolve the sugar in ⅔ cup water, add the chopped pear, bring to the boil and boil continuously for 10 minutes. Set aside to cool.

2. Once cool, blend the above in a blender until smooth. Stir in the lemon juice.

3. Pour into a plastic container and freeze for 1 hour.

4. After 1 hour, remove the sorbet and beat it well with a fork. Incorporate the beaten egg white gently, using a metal spoon.

5. Cover and return to the freezer until needed.

SERVING IDEA   Make fruit coulis (fruit sauce) by blending fruit in a blender and adding a little sugar. Pour this sauce over the sorbets.

FREEZER TIP   Any of the sorbets can be made in advance and stored in the freezer. Remove a few minutes before serving.

☐

OPPOSITE

FRUIT SORBETS

POACHED PEARS IN PORT

A dish to serve either hot or cold; the pears retain the flavor of the port and are absolutely delicious.

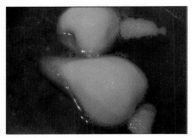

Step 2

□ 4 large pears, peeled □ 2 cups port □ 1 tsp cinnamon
□ Juice of 1 lemon □ 1 heaped cup sugar

1. Pour the lemon juice over the peeled pears – this will prevent them from discoloring.

2. Place the pears in a large saucepan, add the port and just enough water to cover. Sprinkle over the cinnamon and the sugar. Cook on a gentle heat. Test for doneness with the point of a knife.

3. Remove the pears, and either keep warm or chill in the fridge.

4. Put the juice back on a brisk heat and allow to reduce and become slightly syrupy.

5. Pour the sauce over the pears and serve.

TIME   Preparation takes about 5 minutes and cooking takes approximately 1 hour and 20 minutes.

SERVING IDEA   Instead of serving the pears whole, they can be formed into balls using a melon baller.

WATCHPOINT   Watch the juice carefully as it reduces in Step 5, as it tends to reduce quite quickly and will thicken too much if not removed from the heat rapidly.

□

OPPOSITE

POACHED PEARS
IN PORT

—— SERVES 6 ——

PROFITEROLES WITH CHOCOLATE SAUCE

*A great French classic: light choux pastry cases filled with
vanilla ice cream and coated with hot chocolate sauce.*

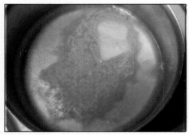

Step 1

Step 2

Step 3

Step 3

□

OPPOSITE

PROFITEROLES
WITH CHOCOLATE
SAUCE

CHOUX PASTRY

□ 1 cup water □ ⅜ cup butter □ Pinch salt
□ 1½ cups all-purpose flour, sifted □ 5 large eggs, beaten

CHOCOLATE SAUCE

□ ¾ cup dark chocolate, melted
□ ½ cup whipping cream □ 2 tbsps sugar

FILLING

□ 2 cups vanilla ice cream

1. In a saucepan, bring the water to the boil, add the butter and the pinch of salt.

2. Remove from the heat as soon as the butter has melted and beat in the flour, a little at a time. Allow to dry out a little.

3. Beat in the beaten egg little by little, retaining a little for brushing, and fill a piping bag fitted with a plain tip with the mixture.

4. Heat the oven to 425°F. Grease 2 cookie sheets, and pipe out 12 small balls of choux pastry, spreading the balls well apart. Mix the remaining beaten egg with a little water and brush over the choux pastry balls.

5. Cook these for 10 minutes and then reduce the heat to 350°F and cook for approximately 20 minutes more – the balls should double in size and be golden brown.

6. Remove from the oven and pierce them to let the steam escape. Turn off the oven, leave the door open, and put the profiteroles back in the open oven to dry out for approximately 10 minutes.

7. Melt the chocolate and the sugar together over a pan of boiling water, then stir in the cream.

8. Slice open the pastry cases, fill with ice cream and pour over the chocolate sauce.

TIME   Preparation takes about 25 minutes and cooking takes 1 hour.

COOK'S TIP   Cut out the base of each choux ball, fill with ice cream and then turn upside down to serve, with the sauce poured over.

WATCHPOINT   Melt the chocolate, cream and sugar over a very gentle heat, stirring continuously, and remove from the heat as soon as the mixture is completely smooth.

—— SERVES 6 ——

BANANAS IN ORANGE SAUCE

The delicious caramel orange sauce makes this a perfect dish hot or cold.

Step 1

Step 1

Step 2

☐ 6 large bananas, peeled   ☐ 3 tbsps sugar
☐ 2 tbsps butter   ☐ 1 tbsp cream sherry
☐ 2 tbsps orange liqueur   ☐ Juice of 2 oranges

1. In a heavy-based saucepan, melt together and then boil the butter and the sugar until a white caramel forms.

2. Stir in the sherry, liqueur and orange juice, and allow the mixture to reduce a little.

3. Cut the bananas into even rounds and add them to the sauce.

4. With a tablespoon, remove the sauce-coated bananas and arrange them on small individual plates. Make rose shapes by interlacing the bananas, then pour over the remaining sauce.

TIME   Preparation takes about 10 minutes and cooking takes 10 minutes.

SERVING IDEA   Presenting the bananas in a rose pattern is, of course, optional, but so much nicer to the eye.

COOK'S TIP   Finely shred about 6 fresh mint leaves and add these just before serving; they give a lovely flavor.

VARIATION   To obtain a really authentic flavor, use French Rivesalts in place of the sherry.

☐

OPPOSITE

BANANAS IN
ORANGE SAUCE

—— SERVES 6 ——

LEMON TART

*Both tangy yet smooth, the lemon filling in this
tart is mouthwateringly delicious.*

SWEET DOUGH

☐ 2 cups all-purpose flour, sifted
☐ ½ cup butter, cut into cubes   ☐ ½ cup sugar
☐ 1 egg, beaten   ☐ Pinch salt

LEMON FILLING

☐ ½ cup butter   ☐ ¾ cup sugar
☐ 5 eggs, beaten   ☐ Juice of 2 lemons   ☐ Zest of ½ lemon

Step 3

Step 3

1. Place the flour in a mixing bowl, add the salt and rub in the butter with your fingers. Stir in the sugar. Mix in the egg and form the dough into a ball. Place in the refrigerator for 5 to 10 minutes.

2. Roll out the dough on a floured surface, line a pie pan with the pastry, and bake unfilled in a moderately hot oven until cooked – approximately 20 minutes.

3. Mix all the ingredients for the lemon filling together in a saucepan. Put over a gentle heat and stir continuously for 10 minutes. The mixture will become quite thick.

4. Allow to cool and chill slightly in the refrigerator. Stir well and then fill the pastry shell. Keep the tart covered in the refrigerator until required.

TIME   Preparation takes about 20 minutes, cooking takes approximately 30 minutes and chilling about 30 minutes.

VARIATION   Use small individual patty shells. The pastry will cook much more quickly – approximately 10 minutes.

SERVING IDEA   Peel a lemon and cut the flesh into thin slices. Remove the pips and place on the finished tart.

☐

OPPOSITE

LEMON TART

---- SERVES 8 ----

CLAFOUTIS AUX CERISES

A mouthwatering cherry and egg dessert,
equally good served hot or cold.

Step 3

Step 3

Step 4

□ 1 cup milk   □ 4 eggs, beaten   □ 3 cups fresh cherries, pitted
□ ½ cup butter   □ ½ cup sugar
□ 2 cups all-purpose flour, sifted   □ 2 pinches salt

---

1. Using a quarter of the butter, grease a large pie pan. Spread the cherries in the bottom of the pan.

2. Bring the milk to the boil in a saucepan, add the salt and allow to cool slightly.

3. Melt the butter, and mix in the sugar, eggs and the flour.

4. Pour the milk into the above sugar/egg mixture, mix well and pour over the cherries in the pie pan.

5. Cook in a moderate oven for approximately 50 minutes.

TIME   Preparation takes about 10 minutes and cooking takes approximately 50 minutes.

SERVING IDEA   Serve the Clafoutis chilled from the refrigerator.

VARIATION   Small, individual flans can be prepared in custard cups, cutting cooking time to about 40 minutes.

□

OPPOSITE

CLAFOUTIS
AUX CERISES

--- SERVES 6 ---

PECHES AU VIN ROUGE

Tender peaches poached in a red wine syrup.

☐ 6 peaches, washed and wiped dry ☐ 4 cups red wine
1½ cups sugar ☐ 1 cup water ☐ 1 stick cinnamon
☐ 1 piece of vanilla
☐ 1 tbsp fresh lemon and orange zest, finely chopped
☐ 1 whole clove

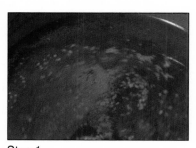

Step 1

Step 2

1. Combine all the ingredients, except the peaches, in a large saucepan and bring to the boil. Allow to boil until the syrup has reduced somewhat and is a little thicker.

2. Put the peaches into the syrup and poach them until they are cooked. Cooking time will depend on the quality of the peaches – test with the point of a sharp knife; there should be just a little resistance.

3. Remove the peaches from the syrup. Allow the syrup to cool slightly. Remove the clove, vanilla and the cinnamon.

4. Slice the peaches and spread out into fan shapes on small individual plates. Pour over the syrup and serve.

TIME   Preparation takes 5 minutes and cooking takes approximately 35 minutes.

SERVING IDEA   Garnish the plates with a few leaves of fresh mint dampened with cold water and the tips dipped in granulated sugar.

TIME SAVER   The peaches and the syrup can be prepared and cooked on the morning of serving and stored separately in the refrigerator. Reheat the sauce slightly just before serving.

☐

OPPOSITE

PECHES AU
VIN ROUGE

--- SERVES 6 ---

TARTE TATIN

A lightly caramelized apple tart that is cooked with the crust uppermost and then turned over on serving.

Step 2

Step 4

Step 4

☐ 1lb flaky pastry ☐ 2 ¼ lbs apples, peeled, halved and cored
☐ ⅓ cup butter ☐ ¾ cup sugar ☐ 3 tbsps heavy cream

1. Dot the base of a pie pan with the butter and sprinkle over half of the sugar.

2. Place the apple halves, rounded side down, onto the butter and sugar, and sprinkle over the remaining sugar.

3. Roll the pastry out into a round just slightly larger than the bottom of the pan.

4. Place the pastry round over the apples, tucking it down at the edges.

5. Cook in a very hot oven 450°F for approximately 30 minutes.

6. Remove from the oven when cooked and turn immediately onto a serving plate.

7. Whip the cream and serve in a small bowl for the guests to help themselves.

TIME   Preparation takes about 15 minutes and cooking takes approximately 30 minutes.

SERVING IDEA   The tart can be served either hot or cold.

VARIATION   If you want a very richly colored caramel, boil together all the sugar and the butter as the first step. When a deep brown caramel has formed, remove it from the heat and pour it rapidly into the pie pan. Then place the apples on top and proceed with Step 3.

COOK'S TIP   Tuck the pastry down well at the edges, so that when you turn the cooked tart over onto the serving plate all the caramel is trapped over the tart.

☐

OPPOSITE

TARTE TATIN

CHOCOLATE MOUSSE

*A favorite throughout France, every chef has his or her
own secret recipe for chocolate mousse. This recipe is easy
to follow and will be much appreciated by all who taste it.*

Step 2

Step 4

□ 2 cups dark chocolate   □ 4 egg yolks, beaten   □ ¼ cup sugar
□ 1 cup whipping cream, whipped until quite thick
□ 4 egg whites, stiffly whipped   □ 4 tbsps warm milk

1. Melt the chocolate in a bowl over a saucepan of hot water. Once the chocolate has melted, stir in the warm milk.

2. Beat the egg yolks with the sugar until white. Stir in the chocolate mixture, mix well and cool for 1 minute.

3. Gently fold in the whipped cream.

4. Then gently fold in the whipped egg whites. Pour the mousse into small individual bowls and set in the refrigerator.

5. Serve cold from the refrigerator.

TIME   Preparation take about 10 minutes, cooking time is about 8 minutes and setting time is at least 3 hours.

SERVING IDEA   Garnish the bowls with a few leaves of fresh mint.

VARIATION   Add the grated zest of a small orange, 1 tsp orange liqueur, or ⅓ cup raisins soaked in 2 tablespoons rum.

□

OPPOSITE

CHOCOLATE
MOUSSE

SERVES 6

GRAPEFRUIT AND WILD STRAWBERRY DUO

*Ligthly poached fresh grapefruit
with a fresh wild strawberry sauce.*

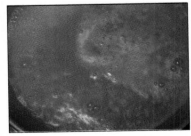

Step 2

Step 2

☐ 5 grapefruit ☐ 2 cups wild strawberries, washed and hulled
☐ 1 cup Muscat wine ☐ ¼ cup sugar

---

1. Peel 4 grapefruits, cut into quarters and squeeze the remaining grapefruit for its juice.

2. In a saucepan, place the Muscat wine and half of the sugar and allow to reduce by half. Add the grapefruit quarters and poach for 1 minute, then remove them using a slotted spoon, and stir in the juice of the 5th grapefruit.

3. Crush the wild strawberries with the remaining sugar, spread this paste over a serving plate, lay the poached grapefruit quarters over this paste and serve the sauce separately in a small serving jug.

TIME   Preparation takes about 35 minutes, and cooking takes about 10 minutes.

VARIATION   Use regular strawberries if the wild variety are not available.

WATCHPOINT   Do not overcook the grapefruit quarters in the syrup; cooking time will depend on the quality of the fruit.

ⒸCopyright F. Lebain.

☐

OPPOSITE

GRAPEFRUIT
AND WILD
STRAWBERRY DUO

—————— SERVES 6 ——————

FRESH FRUIT GRATIN

*Fresh fruit, with a creamy topping,
browned and crisped under a hot broiler.*

☐ ¾ cup confectioner's custard

☐ 2 tbsps kirsch

☐ ¾ cup whipping cream, whipped with ⅛ cup sugar

☐ Seasonal fresh fruit, peeled, pitted, sliced or cubed
(enough for 6 servings)

1. Gently mix together the confectioner's custard, 2 tbsps whipped cream and the kirsch.

2. Using a metal spoon, gently fold in the remaining cream.

3. Arrange the fruit in a pie pan, spoon over the topping and cook for 10 minutes in a moderately hot oven.

4. Transfer to a hot broiler, and allow the top to crisp until brown. Serve immediately.

TIME   Preparation takes about 25 minutes and cooking takes about 20 minutes.

VARIATION   Use a few drops of your favorite liqueur in this recipe instead of the kirsch.

☐

OPPOSITE

FRESH FRUIT
GRATIN

—— SERVES 6 ——

PEACH MELBA

The real peach melba, with fresh raspberry sauce.

Step 1

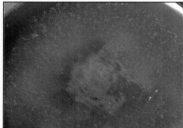
Step 1

Step 2

☐ 6 fresh peaches or canned peaches in syrup
☐ 2 cups vanilla ice cream   ☐ 3 cups fresh raspberries
☐ ¾ cup sugar   ☐ 1 tbsp kirsch   ☐ Juice of ½ lemon

1. In a saucepan, bring to the boil 1 cup water, the sugar, lemon juice, kirsch and the raspberries. Boil briskly for 5 minutes, then set aside to cool.

2. Once cool, blend smooth in a blender, then pass through a fine sieve. Chill in the refrigerator.

3. Place each peach in a small coupe, add a ball of ice cream and pour over a little sauce.

TIME   Preparation takes about 20 minutes and cooking takes approximately 8 minutes. Chill for at least 15 minutes.

VARIATION   Use frozen raspberries if fresh are not in season, and replace the kirsch with different fruit liqueurs.

☐

OPPOSITE

PEACH MELBA

—— SERVES 6 ——

STRAWBERRY MOUSSE
WITH PASSION FRUIT SAUCE

*Called 'Mousse aux Fraises, Coulis Fruit de la Passion,'
this dessert will astound and delight your guests!*

Step 2

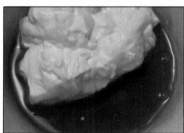

Step 3

Step 3

☐ 3 cups strawberries, washed and drained
☐ 4 passion fruit   ☐ 5 sheets gelatin, pre-soaked
☐ 1 cup sugar boiled with ½ cup water until syrupy
☐ 1 tbsp sugar   ☐ ½ cup cream, whipped

1. Gently heat the syrup in a saucepan with the strawberries. Cook for a few minutes and then blend smooth with a hand mixer or in a blender. Strain through a fine sieve.

2. Add the drained gelatin to the fruit and stir until it has dissolved. Place in the refrigerator to thicken, stirring the mixture from time to time so that it thickens evenly.

3. As soon as the mixture is quite thick, but still liquid, gently fold in the whipped cream. To set the mousse, place in the refrigerator for at least 2 hours.

4. When the mousse is ready to be served, open the passion fruit, scoop out the pulp, including pips, and mix with 1 tablespoon sugar to make the coulis, or sauce.

5. Serve the spoonfuls of mousse with a little passion fruit coulis around the edges.

TIME   Preparation takes about 40 minutes and cooking takes approximately 10 minutes. Chilling and setting time is approximately 3 hours in total.

VARIATION   Use raspberries instead of strawberries.

WATCHPOINT   Don't over-whip the cream as it will turn to butter.

SERVING IDEA   Pour the mousse at Step 4 into small custard cups. Serve either turned out or in the cups.

☐

<u>OPPOSITE</u>

STRAWBERRY
MOUSSE WITH
PASSION FRUIT
SAUCE

———— SERVES 8 ————

FRESH FRUIT IN
RED WINE SYRUP

A lovely summery dessert using as many different fruits as possible, and coated in a red wine sauce.

Step 3

Step 3

☐ 4 cups red wine (Beaujolais or similar)   ☐ 2 cups sugar
☐ ¾ cup water   ☐ 1 whole clove
☐ 1 stick cinnamon   ☐ Zest of 1 orange
☐ A selection of fresh fruit, peeled, pitted, sliced
or halved as necessary

1. Make the syrup by boiling together the wine, water, sugar, whole clove, zest and cinnamon for at least 30 minutes.

2. Remove from the heat and set aside to cool. Chill in the refrigerator.

3. Prepare the fruit and present on a serving dish.

4. Remove the cinnamon and the whole clove. Pour the chilled syrup over the fruit and serve.

TIME   Preparation will take approximately 10 minutes, depending on the fruit you have chosen, and cooking will take at least 30 minutes. Chill for 1 hour.

VARIATION   Once the syrup has chilled, add the fruit and marinate for 1 day in the refrigerator.

WATCHPOINT   Use only very fresh fruit.

SERVING IDEA   Garnish the salad with fresh mint leaves.

☐

OPPOSITE

FRESH FRUIT IN
RED WINE SYRUP

---- SERVES 4 ----

GATEAU GIENNOIS

A nutty-flavored, fluffy-topped tart, with a surprise raspberry center.

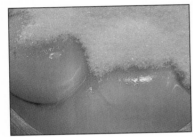

Step 2

Step 4

Step 5

☐ 1½ cups shortcrust pastry   ☐ 3 egg yolks
½ cup sugar   ☐ 3 tbsps shelled walnuts, ground
☐ 2 egg whites, stiffly beaten   ☐ 4 tbsps raspberry jam

1. Roll out the pastry on a lightly floured surface. Line 4 individual pie pans with the pastry, pricking the base and sides with a fork.

2. Beat together the egg yolks and the sugar until white.

3. Stir in the ground walnuts.

4. Gently incorporate the beaten egg whites using a metal spoon.

5. Place 1 tbsp of jam in the base of each tart and spoon over the mixture evenly between the 4 tarts.

6. Cook in a moderate oven 350°F until the pastry is cooked and the filling lightly puffed. Serve as soon as possible.

TIME   Preparation takes about 25 minutes and cooking time is approximately 25 to 35 minutes.

VARIATION   Use ground almonds or hazelnuts instead of walnuts.

©Copyright F. Lebain.

☐

OPPOSITE

GATEAU GIENNOIS

SERVES 6

TARTES FINES AUX POIRES

*Tempting tarts consisting of a fine layer of flaky pastry
covered in sliced pears, served with a sweet sauce.*

Step 2

☐ 2 cups flaky pastry   ☐ 4 large pears, peeled, cored and sliced
☐ ½ bottle sweet white wine (Montbazillac if possible)
☐ ½ cup butter, diced   ☐ 2 tbsps sugar

1. Begin by rolling our the pastry and cutting it into 6 even rounds. Place these rounds on 2 lightly-greased cookie sheets.

2. Place the pear slices evenly and decoratively over the pastry. Sprinkle over the sugar.

3. Cook in a moderately hot oven, 350°F, until cooked, brown and crispy – approximately 20 to 25 minutes.

4. In a large, heavy-based saucepan, over a high heat, allow the wine to boil, reduce and thicken.

5. When the wine is syrupy, remove from the heat and stir in the diced butter.

6. Serve the sauce either poured over the tarts or separately in a small sauce boat.

TIME   Preparation takes about 10 minutes and cooking takes 35 minutes.

SERVING IDEA   Serve with a ball of pear sorbet, and garnish with fresh mint.

COOK'S TIP   Serve the sauce as soon as you have added the butter, and don't let the sauce get cold.

☐

OPPOSITE

TARTES FINES
AUX POIRES

—— SERVES 4 ——

POMMES SAUTEES
AU MUSCAT

Sautéed apples with currants.

Step 1

Step 2

Step 2

☐ 4 Golden Delicious apples, peeled and quartered
☐ ¼ cup butter   ☐ 3 tbsps currants
☐ ½ cup Muscat   ☐ ¼ cup sugar   ☐ 1 tsp cinnamon

1. Melt the butter in a large frying pan, sauté the apples, add the sugar and allow to caramelize slightly.

2. Sprinkle over the currants and cook for a few seconds more.

2. Deglaze the pan with the Muscat, sprinkle over the cinnamon and serve immediately.

TIME   Preparation takes about 5 minutes and cooking takes approximately 10 minutes.

COOK'S TIP   Soak the currants in a cup of tea (without milk), draining before using.

WATCHPOINT   The frying pan should not be returned to the heat once it has been deglazed.

SERVING IDEA   Serve with a glass of chilled Muscat.

VARIATION   Substitute the Muscat with a sweet white wine.

☐

OPPOSITE

POMMES SAUTEES
AU MUSCAT